The Time of My Life

To Dr Michelson

a great Doctor
that I enjoy
visiting ...
    Best wishes
    Jack Leonard

The Time of My Life

JACK LEONARD

Leonard, Jack.
    The time of my life.
I. Title.
    1. Autobiography
Library of Congress Catalog Card Number 93-74776
ISBN 0-9639900-0-4

To the Leonard boys:
(Jack, Mike, Tim and Kevin)

If only you—my four boys—read these memoirs, I will be satisfied. This story will give you an idea how I spent my youth and my working hours and why I was away from home so frequently.

Having not had the luxury of a file of press clippings to refer to, I have taken it upon myself to tell you my story and in my own words. Every word is from memory—I had no reference tapes or notes. The people with whom I associated, both as a child and as an adult, left such an indelible mark that notes were not required. I could never forget them or the experiences we shared.

I just talked into a hand held tape recorder and the material flowed. Yes, I did check on some dates and facts to be as accurate as possible.

You boys were so good and so helpful growing up—you made the job of being a father easy. I thank you.

Also, you married great girls and are doing a wonderful job of raising your families. That's why God put us on earth—to perform to the best of our abilities.

Thanks again for everything—I would not change places with anyone in the world. Why? Because you fellows made my life great. Thanks,

Spoose

Contents

Foreword

Jack Leonard is an Irish-American, old fashioned patriot who has written a gem filled with joyous reminiscences of a life filled with adventure and love of family and country. Jack's enthusiasm, talent, and charm enabled him to have many careers, experiences, and challenges in publishing, real estate, advertising, philanthropy and marketing. He and Marge raised four thriving sons and the Leonard Family reunions are packed with good humor, love, and respect. Jack's memories give the reader better understanding of American history in the 20th Century— because Jack enriched many parts of American life.

—Newton N. Minow

(Mr. Minow is a former chairman of the Federal Communications Commission—1961-63—and is currently of Counsel, Sidley & Austin, Chicago, Ill.)

Acknowledgements

It may sound trite, but I really had the time of my life writing "The Time of My Life." Once I started on this project, the names and stories from years ago came back to life. It was like they occurred yesterday. It really brought back some special memories.

I guess my first thank you should go to my Olympus cassette recorder for holding up during this project. Every story which appears in this book was first told on tape. It all came from the top of my head. I did not have the luxury of notes or files in which to refer. However, the people that I have encountered in my life were so special that it would be difficult to forget them.

I would like to thank my collaborator, Sid Shapira, for the endless hours spent on this project and for enduring the agony of listening to my countless stories.

Many thanks to Newton N. Minow for taking time out from his busy schedule to write the foreword.

I would also like to thank our typesetter, Rose Mario-Gourley, for her diligent work and technical advice.

Thanks to our printer, Phil Oels, for his professional advice and for keeping to our tight schedule.

Thank you to Sheila Shapira-Cortez for her artistic talents in designing a first-class book cover.

And, finally, a sincere thank you to everyone who has purchased this book. I hope you enjoy reading it as much as I enjoyed writing it.

Jack

1

"The Best Job in the United States"

The year was 1951 and the place was Chicago. Chuck Hanson, my friend and colleague at Time Inc., and I were driving along Lake Shore Drive about three miles north of the Loop. We were talking shop—you know, discussing things that had crossed our desks, recent business trips we had made, that sort of thing. After a few minutes, Chuck turns to me and says:

"You know, Jack, you and I have the best jobs in the United States of America. Can you imagine working under better conditions? The freedom we have, the responsibility we have—not to mention the pay we receive, the perks we get and the atmosphere we work in. Can you imagine anything better?"

No, I couldn't. That statement had such a profound impact on me. And, Chuck was absolutely right. In my mind, when I was with Time Inc.—even though there were times when you'd have the odd run-in—the company itself was the greatest place for anyone to work.

The special thing about working at Time Inc. was that it

was so democratic. You felt as though you were not only welcome, but part of a team. From top to bottom, it was the same. Whether they knew your name or not the first time they saw you, they learned it quickly and treated you with dignity and respect.

I remember the first time I met the president of Time Inc., Roy Larsen. He introduced himself as Roy. I was Jack and that's the way we went on for the rest of the time. As high as they might be, they treated the lowest man on the totem pole with as much dignity as possible.

Then, there was the founder of Time Inc., Henry R. Luce, or Harry as he preferred. He showed his respect in subtle ways. For example, when he was on an elevator with four other people and he only knew three of them, he would say nothing at all. He did not want to embarrass or insult the one whose name he did not know.

For me, I considered it a great blessing to be able to work alongside people like Roy Larsen, Harry Luce and the rest of the original group at Time Inc. They taught me the business and I'm forever grateful. It was an honor to be part of the second generation at Time Inc. The third and fourth generations that are there now never knew Roy Larsen, Harry Luce, Charlie Stillman, Howard Black, Nick Wallace, Chuck Hanson, Clay Buckhout, Sid James, Bob Heiskell et al. My good fortune and their loss. These originals were, without a doubt, the greatest people—in life and in work— to be around. When I look at Time-Warner today, I know it is not the Time Inc. that I once knew. And, that's too bad.

There was a great sense of family at Time Inc. Everyone

had a genuine concern for the next person. I felt very fortunate in being able to work with some of the giants of publishing such as the aforementioned. They laid the foundation for Time Inc. and they built the company from the ground up. But, more importantly, they had a very human side. They genuinely cared for their colleagues.

When my wife, Marge, gave birth to our son, Tim, in May of 1950, I was attending a *Life* convention in Virginia. They informed me at the convention and Roy Larsen, who was also there, overheard the good news. He quickly called his secretary and before long two dozen tea roses had arrived at my wife's hospital room in Evanston.

Harry Luce had a tradition of sending silver porridge dishes to newborns. Whenever a baby was born in the Time Inc. family, he would present an inscribed dish to the family. For example:

> **TO KEVIN BARRY LEONARD**
> **FROM, HENRY R. LUCE**
> **AND THE REST OF HIS FATHER'S FRIENDS AT TIME INC.**

Needless to say, these kind gestures did not go unnoticed by the Time Inc. staffers.

JACK LEONARD

2

Memories of Paterson

When you grow up during the Depression, you grow up fast. I have fond memories of my childhood in Paterson, New Jersey.

Both my parents emigrated from Ireland. My father, Thomas Joseph Leonard, came from Doocastle, Tubbercurry, County Sligo and he was the first of the Leonard clan to set sail for America. He was only eighteen when he landed at Ellis Island on the SS *Baltic*. He did not know a soul nor did he have a place to go. He settled in Jersey City, N.J. and found employment on the street cars, although the job did not last long. He either ran the car off the track or stayed too long at the St. Patrick's Day parade. That's because it wasn't long before, as he put it, "they asked for my buttons."

Shortly afterwards, my father moved to Paterson, where he worked for the telephone company. It was in Paterson where he met Annie Smith, who had emigrated to America from Drumalee, County Cavan, Ireland in 1908. They were married in 1911. I was born in 1916.

My father was a very hard worker and very reliable. But, he was also known to imbibe on occasion. How we feared the days he would turn to the bottle. He could not take much, but when he started he would go for three or four days—until he got a real good buzz. Then, he would get sick and swear off drinking forever. To this day, I can still hear him in the back room calling out to my mother.

"Annie, I'm dying," he would say.

"Die and be done with it," my mother would reply.

My mother was the most charitable person I have known. I don't think she ever purchased a new dress or coat for herself, but she never refused to help out the next person. As a result, there was always plenty of activity at 14 Pennington Street in Paterson. Our house was marked by the transients—as a good place for a good meal. Nobody was ever turned away. In fact, many of my father's hats and suits went out the door on the heads and backs of strangers—unbeknownst, of course, to my father.

This open-door policy resulted in some unusual circumstances. I can remember the day my mother discovered a strange man sleeping on a bed in one of the rooms of our house. She was flabbergasted. She rushed over to my father to ask him if he knew the man's identity.

My father calmly replied, "No, but we'll ask him when he wakes up." That's the way it was in Paterson. No locks on the doors, no questions asked, nobody turned away. By the way, the stranger ended up living with us for two years.

My father's job at the telephone company meant everything to him. He didn't know the meaning of an eight-hour day. He was always working overtime and his dedication to the company was unwavering.

He would work through blizzards, illnesses, epidemics— you name it. In his days as a troubleshooter for the telephone company, he was often required to perform some unusual duties.

On one occasion, my father had a particularly harrowing experience. There was a break in the line and they discovered it to be inside a water pipe. My father would have to go inside. The water level was lowered to permit my father and a small boat—equipped with a lamp—to enter the pipe. He found the break, fixed it and came out the other end of the pipe, some four miles later. At the time, all he would say about the ordeal was that it was real quiet in there.

Many years later, when the story was reported in the paper, I asked my father why he took on such a dangerous task.

"It was my job," he replied.

You wouldn't find a more dedicated or loyal man than my father.

My father, right,
and I

My parents had four children: in order, Mary, Thomas, myself and Nancy. Unfortunately, Thomas and Nancy both died at a very early age—Thomas at age five from diphtheria and Nancy at age two from scarlet fever.

My big sister, Mary, is five years older than me. She now lives in Erdenheim, Pa., a suburb of Philadelphia. Being my lone sibling, we tolerated each other as best we could when we were growing up in Paterson.

There was no denying Mary's role in the household. She

was the bossy one in the family. She loved to tell everyone what to do—she was the so-called 'chief of the boat.' She set the pace in our household and she found a way to get on our nerves. Specifically, my father and I.

After one incident when Mary pushed her weight around once again, my father turned to me and muttered:

"Oh, if some man would only ask for her hand, I would say yes immediately—regardless of race, creed or color. And, I'll throw in a mink coat to sweeten the deal!"

Don't get me wrong. Mary is a wonderful person, an absolute delight. She is also one of the most generous and considerate individuals you would ever want to meet. But, when I think back to those days in Paterson, I'll never forget my father's humorous remark urging someone to take her off our hands.

I always knew my father to be a very proud person. He was proud of his Irish heritage, but even more so, he was proud to be an American. When he came to visit us in Chicago, he was supposed to stay for two weeks.

One morning, Marge noticed he was packing his suitcase a few days before he intended to return to Paterson. She thought that was odd, so she called me at work.

"Did you and your father have a fight?" asked Marge.

"Of course not," I replied.

"Well, he's packing his suitcase," she said.

I called my father to the phone and asked him why he was going. It turned out that the next day was election day in

New Jersey and my father wasn't going to miss out.

"I worked hard enough to get my citizenship," said my father. "I'm not going to blow it by not voting this time."

He caught the next train back to New York. My father was able to keep his perfect record intact. He never missed a vote.

Paterson, N.J. was known as the silk capital of the country in the 1920s and 1930s. There were other industries in town such as iron works and machine shops, but silk was the most prominent industry at that time.

We lived in a middle-class neighborhood on Pennington Street. Many of the homes there were two-family dwellings. That is, the homeowners lived on the second and third floors and rented out the first floor to help pay the bills.

Our house was situated near the hub of activity in the community. A block away was the Paterson Armory and across the street from the Armory was the No. 6 Firehouse.

The Armory was the center of the social/sports activity in Paterson. Any event of any consequence was held there—auto shows, food shows, basketball games, fights, and track meets.

The Paterson Crescents were part of a professional basketball league with teams from Cleveland, Brooklyn and Fort Wayne. The league was definitely unique, although at the time we didn't think so.

The games were played in a net, with no out of bounds. The players would go through one end of the net and when a substitution was made they would have to unleash the net to let the substitute enter the game. Each team had its own star player and the players would get a maximum of $50 cash per game, payable in advance. All of the players held jobs during the day.

The Paterson star was Bennie Borgeman, who was also a pretty fair shortstop for the Rochester Triple A club. Fort Wayne's standout player was Fatty Banks, while Cleveland had Joe Lapchick and Brooklyn had the Brennan brothers.

The games were held mainly on Saturday nights. Instead of mascots and slam-dunk competitions, these games would feature an orchestra and dancing at half-time and after the game. As difficult as it is to imagine, this league was to be the forerunner to the NBA.

Like many of the kids in the neighborhood, I competed in Golden Gloves boxing. This was our main form of recreation and we all had a lot of fun. Most of us were knocked out early, but the few who had some talent managed to last a couple of weeks.

Each boxer had to supply his socks, shoes, and athletic supporter. The *Paterson Evening News* and the Patrolmen's Benevolent Association were the co-sponsors of the event and they provided us with two sets of robes and trunks— one red and one blue. The trunks were for all divisions—one size fits all, or so they thought. For the little guys, the trunks extended well below the knees. Meanwhile, for the heavyweights the trunks resembled jockey shorts.

Still, the cost of purchasing boxing shoes (about $4.50) was too steep for many of us. We approached Jake Breslin, a local politician and promoter, and asked him to help us out. He agreed to buy the shoes for us, with one stipulation. He insisted that we put the initials "JB" on the soles of the shoes—"J" on one sole, "B" on the other. Then, in case you were knocked out or knocked down, the photographer would have a chance to take your picture with Jake Breslin's initials on the soles of your feet. Jake must have had an idea we'd be spending plenty of time on the canvas.

A local newspaper photographer, Izzie Schwartz, was hired by Jake to take pictures at the fights. Izzie had a bad leg and Jake had him limping around the ring all night long trying to get the perfect shot as the boxers fell to the canvas.

There were some twenty fights a night and we were getting dizzy just watching Izzie circle the ring on his bad leg whenever one of Jake's fighters was in the ring. How was this guy to know which way we would fall? By the end of the evening, Izzie was exhausted. Believe me, the fighters didn't get half the workout Izzie did.

One of the better athletes in our neighborhood was a guy named Lou Cristello. His father was our insurance salesman. Lou was a natural—he could do anything he wanted to do. In fact, in high school he won the state free throw shooting competition.

Like most of us in the neighborhood, Lou loved boxing. We would often spar at each other's houses. I remember one day when my mother was having tea over at the Breslin's house. Lou came racing up the stairs and asked Mrs. Breslin for a bucket of water.

"What happened, Lou?" inquired Mrs. Breslin. "Why do you need the water?"

Lou replied: "Midgey Shields just got knocked out and I have to throw this on him to wake him up."

Just another typical day in Paterson. Lou and his friends having some fun in the Breslin's basement.

Unfortunately, Lou was never able to get past the first year of high school. That's because every January he would leave to go on the burlesque circuit. However, it was—as they say—a good career move. Lou Cristello, better known as Lou Costello, would soon appear on the Kate Smith show with partner Bud Abbott doing their hilarious "Who's on First" routine. A brilliant career in showbiz was about to take off.

After he made his very successful "Buck Privates" movie, we decided to have a day for Lou. Bill Durkin and I organized the affair, which was preceded by a parade. Every celebration in Paterson had to include a parade. It was going to be quite an event—even a street was going to be named after Lou.

We had made all the arrangements but we still didn't know what to give Lou. We didn't have the money to buy him a lavish gift. Then, somebody came up with the perfect gift idea—an honorary high school diploma.

In planning this affair, we decided we should offer some form of entertainment. Bill Durkin remembered seeing a comedian perform at a recent dance marathon in East Paterson. Bill went to see this upstart comedian and offered him the chance to entertain at Lou's dinner. The comedian accepted the offer and was a big hit. The young comedian's name—Red Skelton.

In 1936, we were going to play a baseball game in Annapolis, Md. Driving through Baltimore en route to Annapolis, we noticed the marquee on the Gaiety Burlesque House featured Abbott and Costello.

By this time, all my friends at Mount St. Mary's College knew of my association with Lou. We would have to catch the show. We asked our coach, Art Malloy, if we could eat in Baltimore after the game. He approved and issued each of us two dollars in meal money. Of course, the money was not to be spent on food, but rather on admission to the burlesque show.

Our seats were very close to the stage and I was determined to get Lou's attention while he was performing. I coughed and made other audible sounds—"psst, psst"—throughout the show, hoping to catch his eye. To his credit, Lou continued on without interruption. But, as soon as he left the stage, he peered through the curtain to see who the jerk was who was making all the commotion. When he saw who it was, he motioned for me to come backstage. Of course, my friends followed me step for step. There we were, students of a fine, upstanding Catholic college backstage at a burlesque show.

Naturally, news of this episode spread quickly throughout the campus after we returned home and we were subsequently disciplined. For the next two weeks, we were confined to the campus.

Even after all his success in Hollywood, Lou Costello never changed a bit. He was the same ol' Lou—just one of the guys. He'd return to Paterson after he had become a star and bang on your door asking if you wanted to go to the Giants' game. During half-time of basketball games, Lou would be out there shooting baskets with the rest of the kids.

When I was working for Time Inc., I had to go to Los Angeles on business. We were going to open a new plant out there and I was to meet with a fellow named George Diehl, who was in charge of production at the Los Angeles office.

When I arrived in Los Angeles, George picked me up and drove me to his house. En route, I started telling him stories about my childhood and one of my chums, Lou Costello. George's ears immediately perked up. George had two young daughters, both of whom were suffering from cystic fibrosis.

George asked me if we might be able to see Lou. I told him I didn't have Lou's number. He said that would be no problem as they had all of the unlisted numbers at the office. So, we stopped at the office and got Lou's number. I called Lou and he insisted that we come over for a visit. We went back to George's house to pick up his wife and two children.

Lou couldn't have been more gracious. He was so good to those children—showing them movies, making them lunch and entertaining them all day long. The kids were in heaven, spending a day with a Hollywood star. I didn't even have a chance to inform Lou about their illness until later.

Meanwhile, after we had been there for a while, Lou comes into the room and says to me: "Somebody wants you on the phone."

I turned to him and replied: "Lou, how could that be? I don't know anybody in Los Angeles!"

So, I went into the bedroom to pick up the phone and it's my father on the line from Paterson. Lou had sneaked off and called my father and told him that "Jackie was here and he'd like to speak to you."

That's the kind of guy Lou Costello was.

After graduating from Mount St. Mary's College in Emmitsburg, Md. with my business degree in 1939, I landed my first job. It was with The Great Atlantic & Pacific Tea Company. They opened the very first supermarket in Passaic, N.J. located at 167 Jefferson Street. (I was familiar with the area having worked at the Jefferson Street crossing for the Erie Railroad for three summers. The pay was $68 per month, twelve–hour shifts, seven days a week.) At my permanent job at A & P, I was to be paid $16 a week, cash, and was sent to the Butter and Bacon warehouse. I was thrilled to have a steady job and to be able to earn some real money. So, when I received my pay after my first week of work, I couldn't wait to open the envelope. I ripped it open, only to find there was just $11 in there.

When I questioned my boss, Walter Riley, about being shortchanged, he asked me if I worked on Monday. I said I hadn't worked because it was a holiday. You don't get paid for holidays, was Mr. Riley's terse reply.

I did manage to make a positive impression on my bosses at A&P, however. I had noticed that when new employees started at the store, it took them a while to learn the ropes. I suggested the company implement training sessions for new employees at a 'fake' store in the warehouse. Then, when the newcomers were sent out to the real stores, they'd know what they were doing. My bosses adopted this idea. Not long after, I left the company to join the Navy in 1941.

When I was first called to active duty in May 1941, I learned my duties in a relaxed atmosphere. Not many reserves were called to active duty at the time and it was anything but a mob scene at Third Naval District Headquarters (90 Church Street) in New York City. In fact, we weren't even required to wear a uniform.

Nevertheless, I noticed that almost all the other reserves were dressed the same way. They wore J. Press suits. I soon discovered that most of these reserves were from the Yale University Naval ROTC program.

(The boys from Yale, nonetheless, made an impression on me. The first thing I did after being discharged from the Navy in late 1945 was to go to New Haven, Conn. and purchase a J. Press grey flannel suit. Just maybe it helped me get the job at Time Inc.)

Anyway, not long after I arrived at Third Naval District Headquarters, Walter Winchell, the celebrated gossip columnist for the *New York Daily News*, was called to active duty. I thought he was a nice guy, although many of the other officers were suspicious of him. Thus, Walter had a brief stay before he was returned to inactive status. Apparently, there were widespread fears that sensitive information could be leaked through his column, which he continued to write while on active duty.

Nevertheless, while Walter was on active duty, he was given a special assignment. He was to promote the Joe Louis-Buddy Baer heavyweight championship fight in early January, 1942. Proceeds from the fight would go to Navy relief.

The day after the fight—which Louis won in a first round knockout—the champ came to the Navy offices with his handlers to present the Navy relief check to Admiral Adolphus Andrews. Since everything had to be logged though the duty office—where I was located—I was soon introduced to Joe Louis. He was such a magnificent specimen. Dressed in a Glen Plaid suit, he looked like a million bucks.

I gladly accepted the check—in the amount of $119,000 for Navy relief—from Louis. Before he left, we conducted a publicity stunt—a mock weigh-in. Joe weighed in at 215 pounds, compared to 208 at the time of the fight. Buddy Baer unexpectedly arrived at our office that day and admitted he was surprised with the outcome of the fight.

"I thought I could take him," said Buddy. "He was so small, he only came up to my chin. The problem was, he came up to my chin too frequently!"

While on duty one afternoon, someone came into the office and told me to look out the window. All I could see was a blanket of smoke over the Hudson River.

The USS _Normandie_ was on fire. It was the biggest luxury ship afloat at the time and the Navy had taken it over. They were in the process of converting it into a troop ship.

I was working in the office until midnight that day. At about 6:30 p.m., I received a phone call from Lt. Ernest Lee Jencke, Admiral Andrews' aide. Lt. Jencke asked me to get him the time of high tide and low tide at Pier 52. I went over to get the tide tables, not knowing exactly what to do. I went back to the phone and relayed the information to Lt. Jencke:

"6:12 a.m. and 6:12 p.m.—high and low tide," I said.

When I returned to work for my shift the next morning, I noticed an alarming sight on the bus ride over. I looked out the window and saw the USS _Normandie_ laying on its side like a big, wounded whale in the middle of the Hudson River.

I immediately thought I had given Lt. Jencke the wrong time of high tide and that caused the ship to capsize. I was scared to death. Thoughts of being court marshalled, flogged, tarred and feathered went through my mind. I could only think of the worst possible scenario. I was convinced an erroneous tide time had caused this catastrophe.

I decided I'd better call the office. If they answered the phone in a friendly manner, I would tell them I was on my way. But, if they sounded hostile, I'd tell them I was sick in bed, waiting for the doctor to arrive. What a relief it was when they answered in a cheerful tone. I told them I'd be there in five minutes.

It turned out that they had scuttled the ship to put out the fire. If they left it where it had been, the fire could have

Marge and I just after I had been discharged from the Navy— she's the pretty one

caused severe damage. History has said that the fire was a blessing. The ship was outfitted to carry 10,000 troops and it would have been a marked target for Hitler's U-boats.

Nevertheless, those fifteen minutes from the time I saw the *Normandie* on its side until the time I called the office were the most stressful of my life. I was sure my Navy days were over.

I certainly had my share of excitement while at the Third Naval District Headquarters.

One particular Sunday, I had the Duty from 9:00 a.m. until midnight. It was a quiet day and I can recall spending it reading the paper and listening to the New York Giants-Brooklyn Dodgers football game on the radio. Suddenly, standing in front of me was a radio man—1st class. He was as white as a sheet and he was clearly shaken. He handed me a typed memo. It said: "Execute W.P.L. 46 against Japan."

I was stunned. It was like I was shot. We were going to war! The radio shack started to buzz. Teletype machines were clicking up a storm. Not much later, the local radio stations were broadcasting the attack on Pearl Harbor.

What a spot to be put in! I was alone so I could not leave my station for any reason. So, I pulled out the Navy roster and, starting with Admiral Adolphus Andrews, I began calling every head of every department in the Third Naval district and had them report to their station—immediately.

The phones started to ring. People appeared from

nowhere. Old retired sailors called and wanted to report for duty. Sailors on leave called to ask for instructions. Report to your ship or station immediately, they were told.

Admiral Andrews was not at his headquarters at the Brooklyn Navy Yard. He was somewhere between Syosett, Long Island and the Navy Yard. I notified the New York Police Department and told them to intercept the admiral's car and have him report to headquarters. They did.

I worked all night long and was relieved at about 8:00 a.m., Monday, December 8th, 1941. Before I signed out, I was asked to report to Captain McKinney, chief of staff. He asked me to give him a verbal report on what I had done. Then, I was sent into Admiral Andrew's office. Again, I reported what steps I had taken. When I finished, he gave me the Navy "well done" as had Captain McKinney before him. The "well done" was put into my Navy file.

A long day—"a day that will go down in infamy"—was over. An article was written some time later entitled:

"Going to war with an ensign." I might also add, a green one.

After the war, I returned to Paterson in late 1945 and rejoined The Great Atlantic & Pacific Tea Company. I was in the real estate department, selecting new locations for stores. I was paid $26 a week. This position lasted all of two weeks. That's because I was to receive an offer from Harry Faeber to join Time Inc., with an opportunity to earn $5,000 a year. At four times the salary I was presently making, it was an offer I couldn't refuse.

Still, there were those such as A&P vice-president, Allan Burtis, who questioned my logic.

"Publishing?" wondered Burtis. "That comes and goes. No security. But, the food business—everyone must eat. It's a long-term business."

Security was the key buzzword back then. After all, it was more desirable to work for a large, secure company (General Electric, the telephone company, the post office) rather than risk joining a publishing company.

3

"Jack of All Trades"

"Jack of all trades." That should have been my nickname during my early years at Time Inc. in New York. When I first started out in 1946, I was working in the corporate production department under Harry Faeber. I was helping out with the mail, doing all the chores required of a newcomer.

My experience as a lieutenant commander in the Navy didn't count for much when I applied for the job at Time Inc. When they asked me what I could do, I replied that I could navigate and read flashing lights. My two and a half stripes didn't mean much. But, I wasn't alone. There were a lot of guys in the same boat, so to speak.

Basically, I started as a glorified office boy. We were known as CB/OBs—college boys/office boys. In a roundabout way, my college experience gave me my first break at Time Inc.

One night when I was working late, I bumped into Jim Ainslie. Jim, who worked as an assistant to the vice-president of production, had just come out of a meeting. I asked him what was going on. He said he was working on his budgets, but he didn't have all the necessary costs.

"We know the price of paper, the price of ink, and everything else, but we don't have any idea of what the postal rates will be," said Jim.

I quickly seized the opportunity. "Well, I know Joe Joe Lawler."

Joe Joe had been my college baseball coach but, more importantly, he was now third assistant postmaster general in the Truman administration and handled magazines and that type of material.

Jim Ainslie turned around and headed right back into the meeting with Dave Brumbaugh, his immediate supervisor. A few moments later, Jim retrieved me from the hallway and asked me to come into the room. Dave Brumbaugh asked me how well I knew Joe Joe and if I could call him.

I called Joe Joe at his home in Washington, D.C. We reminisced and talked about our experiences in the war. He asked me what I was doing now.

"Joe, I'm working for Time Inc. and they're working on their budgets now," I said. "They need to know what the postal rates will be and they want to meet with you."

"I'm in the office all next week," said Joe. "How about next Tuesday?"

I checked with Dave and Jim and they nodded in agreement. When I hung up the phone, I told my colleagues that Joe Joe wanted me to be at the meeting in Washington. He didn't say anything of the sort, but I wasn't going to pass up the chance of a free trip to Washington with some of the top executives at Time Inc.

The next Tuesday, I boarded a train with the top brass en route to Washington. We arrived at Joe's office and received the good news that there would be no postal rate increase during that administration. I became an instant hit with my colleagues.

When I returned to New York, there was news of a job opening in Chicago. When the news crossed a colleague's desk, I overheard someone say, "they should give it to the kid that went to Washington with us."

The post office incident gave me instant credibility and I'm certain it paved the way for my promotion and move to Chicago. You've got to take advantage of any opportunity that comes your way and I often wonder what would have happened had I not bumped into Jim Ainslie in the hallway that night.

My last assignment in production before joining Doc Wooley at _Life International_ was just another in a line of enlightening experiences at Time Inc.

Dave Brumbaugh allowed me the opportunity to arrange and assist in moving the _Fortune_ press from Jersey City Printing to Donnelly in Chicago. It was a monumental task.

It was time to put on overalls and prepare for the move. I discovered that you can learn a great deal by observing others. And, that's exactly what I did.

The planning and detail work involved in this move was quite astounding. Every bolt, screw, and roller belonging to this humongous machine had to be inventoried, wrapped, marked, and stored. That's because the last item up—the bed plates—would be the first item installed at the new location.

I truly marvelled at the skills of these gifted engineers and mechanics. The manner in which this operation was executed was remarkable. Even the route the trucks would take from New Jersey to Chicago was carefully mapped out. The turns on the roads were measured, as were the heights and clearances of the underpasses. The entire operation ran so smoothly and was so well coordinated. Which goes to show that the brains of an operation aren't the exclusive property of the ones in suits.

Success depends on ability and cooperation of craftsmen and good labor. The suits get the credit, but they need the help of the foot soldiers and they should always be grateful. You can draw an analogy of a football team. The quarterback is the one who gets all the accolades, but how successful would he be without a lot of help up front.

For me, this experience reinforced the notion that success is the by-product of teamwork. I'm grateful to Dave Brumbaugh for including me in this operation.

At Time Inc. we learned the art of being resourceful. That was never more evident than in 1946. That year, there was a nationwide coal strike which threatened to disrupt our operations. The strike meant that our plants would be working on a limited basis. Consequently, production of our magazines—_Time, Life, Fortune, Architectural Forum, House and Home_—would be in severe jeopardy.

However, the strike didn't matter one bit to our advertisers. All that mattered to them was our getting these publications in the hands of millions of subscribers.

Charlie Stillman, our vice-president of corporate operations, thought he could solve this problem by buying excess army machinery at Camp Mead, N.J. Charlie heard they had some gas generators there and he arranged to purchase 50 KW gas generators and 10-500 KWs. I accompanied Charlie and other executives out to Camp Mead to inspect the generators.

Once these generators had been purchased, there was the problem of getting them to Chicago. The coal strike had curtailed train traffic, so Charlie worked out a deal with Pennsylvania Railroad. He purchased a freight train, 10 flat cars, an engine and a caboose to carry the generators to Chicago. I soon found out why I made the trip to Camp Mead. I was to hop on the caboose and accompany the equipment on the trip west. Charlie handed me a fistful of blank Western Union telegram slips with the instructions to keep him updated as we—the generators and I—made our way to Chicago.

Charlie then hired a large trucking company to meet us at the docks when we arrived to coordinate delivery of the generators to our various printers. Operation Stillman was in full swing.

Just one thing—in the middle of this grandiose operation, it was announced that the coal strike was over. We wouldn't be needing the generators after all. When Charlie was advised of this development, he promptly turned around and sold the generators to Mexico—at a profit! Charlie Stillman was a genius, pure and simple.

I soon found out that besides being a genius, Charlie was also an appreciative, generous individual—following the blueprint set forth by other Time Inc. executives. When I returned to work after my journey on the train—which I enjoyed immensely—Charlie called me into his office. He asked me to provide him with a full verbal and written account of the operation.

Then, he called in his secretary, Libby Armstrong, and asked her to run down to the bank to cash a check for him. Before long, Libby returned and gave the money to Charlie.

Charlie smiled and then turned to me: "I understand your wife is about to give birth (to son, Jack). I hope this will help you out. With my personal compliments."

Charlie then proceeded to hand me ten crisp $100 bills. I was overwhelmed. It was the first time I had ever seen $1,000 all at once. That's the way it was at Time Inc. They really cared about their employees.

Working for Charlie Stillman, you never knew what kind of assignment you were going to get from day to day. That was part of the excitement and intrigue in working for Time Inc.

One day, my friend Wes Pullen and I were given an unusual task. We were asked to check up on the residents of the Margery Hotel in New York. Time Inc. had an option to buy the hotel at 49th Street and Park Avenue, across from the Waldorf Astoria. The plan was to make this building the site of the new Time and Life Building.

Wes and I began to check the lists to find out who the tenants were. We soon realized that many of the residences belonged to people who headed up prominent companies. And, these companies were very good customers of our magazines.

However, the occupants of the building were not paying the rent directly. Some sugar daddies—and well-known sugar daddies, at that—were responsible for that.

Well, we took our findings back to Charlie at the office. How could we possibly tell these people they would have to move out? Clearly, we'd alienate some of our best customers and lose plenty of advertising revenue.

In the end, Time Inc. made a wise business decision and decided to look elsewhere for a location. The location they found is now the Time Life Building at 6th Avenue and 50th Street in New York.

Time Inc. begins printing on the West Coast at Pacific Press in Los Angeles in the early 1950s. Back row, left to right: *Harry Caywood, Wayne Crotty, Frank Mulford, Jack Leonard, Nick Wallace. Front row,* left to right: *Bill Clum, George Diehl*

One night, a bunch of us were on the train discussing the future of Time Inc. We were speculating on who might be the next president of the company. Charlie Stillman received everyone's support, save one.

Like all of us, Ralph Lewis had great respect for Charlie. However, he had some reservations.

"Charlie could make nine great decisions for the company," reckoned Lewis. "But, the tenth one might sink the company. So, he always needed somebody to say no."

For years, *Life* magazine was only printed in Chicago and Philadelphia. This created problems with our distribution on the West Coast. By the time the magazines were shipped to the West Coast, we had lost two days on the newsstands. Naturally, this did not please our advertisers.

Charlie Stillman decided that we should alleviate this dilemma by printing on the West Coast. I was sent to Los Angeles to oversee the installation of the *Time* and *Life* presses at our new printer, Pacific Press. My instructions were simple—stand guard on the Pacific Press floor and make sure nobody was sitting down on the job. Charlie told me to put on some overalls and look like I knew what I was doing. Putting on the overalls was no problem, but looking like I knew what I was doing was another story.

While I was in Los Angeles, I stayed at the Beverly Hills Hotel. When I told the room clerks—most of whom were struggling actors—that I was from Time Inc., they assumed I was a writer. Little did they know that I was spending my days on the press floor. When I left for work in the morning, I'd be wearing a business suit. Upon arriving at the plant, I'd change into overalls. I'd change back before returning to the hotel.

One night, I noticed a large crowd in the hotel lobby. I asked the room clerk what was going on. He told me it was for the *Look* movie awards and he suggested I attend. I reminded him that I worked for a rival and that it might not be such a great idea.

"Don't worry," he said. "Just wear a dark suit, white shirt and a bow-tie and walk in. They'll think you're a waiter."

So, when the lights went down and the band struck up a military march, I tried to blend in with the 'real' waiters, by carrying a cake on a platter with a towel draped over my arm. I quickly dropped the tray and the towel and found the first available seat. Occupying the seat beside me was a young starlet looking to be discovered—Dinah Shore.

When I went to the men's room during the evening, I found myself washing hands next to Gregory Peck, who had received the best actor award. A photographer walked in and said he had the perfect picture—one of me congratulating Gregory Peck. All I could think of was the picture showing up in *Look* and me working for *Life*. I excused myself and made a dash for the exit.

"Not quite in the Nick of time"

In the fall of 1947, I was browsing one afternoon at that famous New York landmark, F.A.O. Schwartz. For those of you not familiar with F.A.O. Schwartz, it is one of the most incredible toy stores you'll find anywhere. Kids and adults flock to the store to view the latest merchandise and displays. It's a place where you can easily lose track of time. Unfortunately, that happened to me that afternoon.

While I was in the store that day, a photographer from *The Saturday Evening Post* asked me if I wouldn't mind posing for a few pictures. He was doing a photo spread for the Christmas issue of the magazine. I was only too happy to oblige.

I couldn't wait for the issue to appear on the newsstand. Every week, I would rush to the newsstand to see if my photos were in the magazine. When the Christmas issue of *The Saturday Evening Post* finally came out, I picked up a bunch of copies and rushed back to the office. I plopped the issue on Nick Wallace's desk and asked him to turn to the article on toys. Nick did so and immediately noticed the photos of me at the toy store.

Nick had a very gruff demeanor and he was proud of it. Intimidation was part of his game. He looked up and gave me one of his menacing stares.

"You, son of a bitch! I oughta fire you," he barked.

"Why, I didn't do anything wrong," I explained. "The guy just asked me if he could take a couple of pictures. It doesn't say I work for the competition (*Life*)."

"Look at the clock in each picture," he snapped. "Since when does a clerk take a two-hour, lunch hour."

He had me there. There were four photos of me in the store. There was also a clock in each picture, starting at 12:30 and ending at 2:30 P.M. Leave it to Nick to spot that and ruin what had been a perfectly good day.

Any occasion seemed to be a good occasion for a party at Time Inc. I was glad I decided early in life not to drink. I was the so-called 'designated driver' long before it became in vogue. I would be responsible for making sure my co-workers arrived home safely after the parties. In fact, my colleagues' wives would often call me beforehand to reserve a space in my car. I never came home with an empty car.

Suffice to say, the annual 'Time Outs' parties were quite a celebration, as were the *Life* conventions. The conventions were usually held at first-rate resorts such as Greenbrier in West Virginia or Ponte Vedra in Florida. More than anything else, my first visit to Ponte Vedra was an education in convention attire.

I was surprised to see my colleagues at the convention wearing shorts, knee length socks and loafers. It seemed they were changing outfits for every meeting. Needless to say, I was quite conspicuous wearing long pants from my Navy days.

One day, I was sitting next to Jim Sutherland from the New York office. He wondered why I wasn't in shorts like the rest of them.

I looked at Jim and said: "You know, if I dressed like that in the town I came from, I'd be stoned to death!"

Jim never forgot that line. For the longest time, he kept asking me if I had survived the stonings.

One year, we held a kick-off luncheon to a *Life* convention in Ponte Vedra at the Waldorf Astoria in New York. This gathering was held in New York because scheduling conflicts would not allow many corporate officers to attend the Ponte Vedra convention.

I arrived in New York with the Chicago delegation on Saturday, the day before the luncheon. I rose early the next morning and headed for the 8:00 A.M. Mass at St. Patrick's Cathedral. I waited for the elevator on my floor and when it arrived and the door opened, I was face to face with James A. Farley. Mr. Farley was merely the chairman of the board of Coca-Cola International and former head of the Democratic Party and former postmaster general.

We exchanged greetings and somehow I knew he was headed for the same place as me. The way he was dressed I knew he wasn't going out for a morning jog. So, there I was walking to church with James A. Farley.

When we arrived there, Jim—he was now Jim to me— asked me to join him in his special pew—#1, front row, center aisle. I gladly accepted. Up the aisle we go, me and the General.

There were other *Life* convention-goers at the cathedral and they had noticed me sitting with Mr. Farley. They were obviously taken aback. At the end of Mass, we decide to leave by the side door so as not to cause a stir. Sure enough, my buddies from *Life* made a bee-line to the door, trying to intercept us. I told Mr. Farley that I expected this, so I suggested we ignore them.

When my colleagues met us at the door, I gave them a

quick hello and we kept on walking—no introductions.

Somehow, this incident was relayed to Time Inc. president Roy Larsen. In his speech to the convention, Larsen stressed how important it was to be part of our community and to keep in touch with friends. He went on to say, "Jack Leonard, in from Chicago, had time to get in touch with an old friend, James A. Farley, and because of their busy schedules they arranged to meet for church."

"That's good," said Larsen, not knowing the true circumstances of the meeting.

I remained a good friend of James A. Farley until his death in 1976. We corresponded regularly and I saw him on many of my trips to New York. He rose from New York State Boxing Commissioner to become an advisor to President Roosevelt. He was a wonderful, dignified gentleman who never forgot a name.

In my days at *Life* and *Sports Illustrated*, I worked and socialized with plenty of advertising account executives. Many of them, such as my friend Monty Miller, liked to conduct business over dinner.

One night in the early 1960s when Monty was working at Young & Rubicam as account supervisor on the General Electric—Appliance Division account, about six of us went out for dinner in Detroit. Monty insisted on picking up the tab, as people in his position like to do.

Anyway, the tab came to around $400 and Monty was worried about putting the bill on his expense account. After some thought, he decided to put the expense down as $4,000 and wait for a call from the accounting department. They called and they were flabbergasted.

"$4,000—how could you possibly spend $4,000!" said the accountant.

"Oh, no," replied Monty. "It was only $400."

"Thank you, Monty. Sorry to bother you."

When Monty hung up the phone, he said: "That pill counter thought he just saved the agency $3,600. What a great and thoughtful man I am."

It was such a thrill to be surrounded by such brilliant people at Time Inc.—people like Charlie Stillman and Nick Wallace. An incident during my early days at the New York office underscored their genius.

In the publishing business, paper is obviously a big and expensive requirement. At Time Inc. we worked with all the big paper mills—Mead, International Paper and Champion to name just a few.

Word leaked out that the shipping costs of paper would jump considerably as the railways were threatening to increase their freight charges. This development set the wheels in motion at Time Inc.

Charlie Stillman called a meeting and said we'd have to take steps to solve this problem. Nick Wallace suggested we go over to Staten Island and look at the ships that were for sale. Since I had been in the Navy, he suggested I accompany them to provide some expert insight. I think he just wanted another body to join them on the trip over. We looked at a few freighters over at Staten Island, but found none were conducive to carrying paper.

When we returned to the office, Charlie and Nick decided that we should build our own barges to haul paper from the mills all the way into New York City. We proceeded to build two barges to do nothing but carry paper. They were aptly named the *C. Stillman* and the *N.L. Wallace*. Nick even made the maiden voyage on the barge. The barges were designed to be pushed by a tug through the locks of the canals and towed in open waters.

Charlie had the idea and Nick oversaw the construction and operation of the barges. Their collaboration on this project was magnificent.

Ironically, the railroads never came to us with an increase in freight charges. But, more importantly, we now had the upper hand. We would never be without paper. Because we had our own barges, the railroads would never overcharge us for fear of losing business.

Charlie Stillman was a great man for leverage—not to mention a terrific problem solver.

4

Chicago, Illinois—Second to None

When I was told I was going to be transferred to Chicago in 1948 to work on *Life International*, I was thrilled. I had always enjoyed visiting the city. I had been to Chicago several times—when I was in the Navy and also for Time Inc. when I delivered printing plates to our printer (Donnelly) there.

Once we got there, it didn't take me long to get acclimatized to the new surroundings. My wife Marge, on the other hand, was very homesick. She had lived her whole life on the East Coast and this was quite an adjustment for her. I told my father about the situation and he decided to come out for a visit. He took the train from New York to Chicago.

When I met him at the station, the first thing he said was: "Let's stop at a gas station so I can use the facilities."

You see, he hadn't used the toilet the whole trip. He didn't know the toilet was located under the seat and he was too embarrassed to ask. So, he waited until he arrived in Chicago before using the facilities.

My father had strong Irish roots and one day I took him to a high school football game between New Trier and Vocational of Chicago. My father loved football and it seemed like the perfect way to spend the day.

From the outset of the game, New Trier controlled the ball. They kept giving the ball to a running back named O'Kelly and he was terrific. It was O'Kelly up the middle, O'Kelly around the end, O'Kelly off tackle. O'Kelly was everywhere. He was a one-man team.

Meanwhile, up in the stands, my father is loving every minute of it. At one break in the action, he proudly announces to everyone within earshot: "Well, I guess you need the Irish here, too."

However, midway through the second quarter, O'Kelly goes down with an injury. The trainers come out to examine him and they remove his helmet. O'Kelly is black.

My father immediately turns to me and says: "Let's get outta here." Not because O'Kelly was black, but because my father made so much of the fact he was Irish. He left out of embarrassment.

Chicago, Illinois has many nicknames—the Windy City, the Second City, The City with Broad Shoulders—but, in my mind, it deserves only one handle: "The greatest city in the world."

I fell in love with the city the first time I visited there. I spent some twenty years in Chicago during my years at Time Inc. and they were the greatest years of my life. People are what make a city great and the people of Chicago were exceptional. And, they knew how to put on a party.

Take the 1959 Pan-American Games, for example. In late 1958, I got a call from Art Murphy, the publisher of *Sports Illustrated*. He informed me that Cleveland, which had been awarded the 1959 Pan-Am Games, would be unable to handle them. Art sounded desperate.

"If we lose the Games, it'll be a disgrace to the country," he said. "We wouldn't get another invitation for at least 30 years. Why don't you go down and see your friend, Richard Daley."

I had met the mayor on several occasions and had introduced Art to him earlier that year. The next morning,

I give Mayor Richard Daley, right, of Chicago a Sports Illustrated *pat on the back for the success of the 1959 Pan-American Games.*

I called the mayor's office and made an appointment to see him. I told him that Cleveland would not be able to stage the Games and would Chicago be willing to take them on. That's all I needed to say to the mayor.

"Chicago will take the Pan-American Games," announced Mayor Daley. "Go down and tell one-eyed Riley I said so."

Jack Riley—who had lost an eye and wore a patch over it—was in charge of special events for the mayor. I told Riley the plans. Before I knew it, I was called in for a meeting. What could the city do to help us?

Everyone gave their full support to this project. The University of Chicago, Northwestern and DePaul offered venues and housing. Wrigley Field, Comiskey Park and Soldier Field were lined up as Pan-Am Games venues. Everything came together so quickly.

I suggested we stage sports demonstrations downtown to attract attention for the Games. We were given a strip of prime downtown real estate on Quincy Court to put on these exhibitions. During lunch hours and after work, office workers would be entertained by a variety of activities. We set up a platform and baskets and invited the Boston Celtics to give an exhibition. Bob Richards displayed his pole vaulting skills; there were softball pitchers, high jumpers, jugglers, you name it. Olympic divers Pat McCormick and Sammy Lee gave demonstrations at nearby pools.

Downtown Chicago had been transformed into one giant carnival. It was a sight to behold and these events drew huge crowds to the downtown area. We even invited the Celtics to play a round of golf at North Shore Country Club and sign autographs for the kids.

The Games, themselves, were a huge success and much of the credit had to go to Mayor Richard Daley. Within a few short months after agreeing to bail out Cleveland and save potential embarrassment for the USA, Chicago had staged a most memorable and successful Pan-American Games.

Chicago rolled up its sleeves, went to work and did one helluva job. But then, that shouldn't have surprised me or anyone else living in Chicago.

Speaking of the Reverend Bob Richards, I played a part in arranging his endorsement deal with Wheaties. I had been speaking to some people at General Mills and they wanted to secure some national exposure. They had sponsored baseball for years, but had lost out to the cigarette companies.

I suggested they hire a name athlete and use him as a spokesman. So, they asked me to compile a list of candidates. I gave them a list of twenty-two athletes, including superstars such as Mickey Mantle and Stan Musial. The seventeenth name on the list was Bob Richards, who had gained prominence as a two-time Olympic pole vaulting champion. Nearly everyone else on the list eliminated themselves because of sponsorship deals.

The people at General Mills called me back and said Richards seemed to be their guy, but they were a little afraid of the reverend tag. Bob was an ordained Dunkirk minister.

After some discussion, they decided to go with Bob and the campaign was a huge success. The Reverend Bob Richards went all over the country, preaching the gospel for Wheaties—the breakfast of champions.

Bishop Shiel presents the Catholic Youth Organization fights brought to you by Mogen David Wines. Only Sol Polk could have pulled off that one.

Sol Polk was an outstanding appliance and furniture retailer in Chicago. His operation grew from one store at 2850 North Central Avenue to seventeen stores in the greater Chicago area. He never liked to be called a discounter, although that's precisely what he was. He was the largest independent retailer of General Electric, Westinghouse, Motorola and other national brands. He used to say his only competition was Sears-Roebuck. But, more than anything, Sol Polk was a master promoter.

One year, Bishop Shiel asked Sol to chair the CYO fights in Chicago. Every year, the CYO asked a well-known Chicagoan to serve in that capacity. Sol, being Jewish, was unsure about accepting the role given the religious attachment.

Well, he decided to go ahead. When Sol took on any responsibility, he never did it halfway. He set up an office at the Congress Hotel to run the event and asked many of his friends, including myself, to help out. Sol had no problem getting donations from his suppliers, such as Motorola, General Electric and Whirlpool.

Tickets were selling like crazy. But, Sol didn't want people just to buy tickets and not show up. So, one day we went down to the post office and handed out tickets to all the workers. He wanted to fill Chicago Stadium and that's exactly what he did.

He wasn't through, yet. Sol decided to televise the event locally. It was going to be a first class extravaganza. He arranged a deal with a local station and a top boxing announcer was secured to provide the blow-by-blow action.

Next on the agenda was getting a sponsor for the telecast. That's when Sol came up with Mogen David Wines. And, don't think that didn't get plenty of ink in the papers. The CYO fights brought to you by Mogen David Wines was a huge success.

A few days later, Sol asked me to come up to his office. He said to me: "If a Jewish fellow can run the CYO fights, then an Irish Catholic fellow can wear this."

He presented me with a solid gold St. Christopher medal with a Star of David on the back. He told me to wear it in good health. I'm still wearing it to this day and it's one of my most cherished keepsakes.

Sol Polk was almost bigger than life. His stores had such a high profile in Chicago. Every week, he purchased some twenty-two hours of advertising time on television. Polk Bros. furniture and appliance stores were the talk of Chicago and some people had trouble believing there really was a Sol Polk.

When my son Kevin was born in 1955, I invited Sol to the baptism. Afterwards, Sol went up to the priest who performed the baptism to introduce himself.

He said to the priest: "Hi, I'm Sol Polk."

The priest replied: "Yeah, right. And, I'm George Washington."

♣ ♣ ♣

You'll never meet a more loyal and generous friend than Sol Polk. One day, he asked me how I was doing with the General Electric account. That, of course, was my main account at *Life* magazine. I told him it was going fine. Sol said he was going down to Louisville to meet with Chuck Reiger, vice-president of the appliance division at GE.

Another Sol Polk, right, *promotion at the Wrigley Building*

"Why don't you come down to Louisville that day," said Sol. "I'll be meeting with Reiger about 10 A.M. and when you see me in his office, casually walk by and I'll call you in."

The plan worked to perfection. I walked by the office and Sol calls out: "Oh Jack! Come on in."

He turns to Reiger and says: "Do you know Jack Leonard?"

Reiger said: "Yes, of course. I've had the pleasure."

Sol continued: "You know, Chuck, I couldn't live without your advertising in *Life* magazine. They back it up so tremendously at the point of sale. At my store from door to door, the place is filled with *Life* logos and posters."

That's all I needed. The biggest GE dealer in America is patting *Life* magazine on the back. Obviously, that endorsement from Sol Polk helped to cement *Life*'s relationship with GE for many years. That's the kind of guy Sol Polk was.

On another occasion, a young Polish priest from the West Side of Chicago came to see Sol. It was apparent he was looking for a donation of a range or refrigerator.

Sol said to him: "How is it working for the Pope?"

The priest looked at him with a blank stare: "I've never met the Pope."

"How can you work for somebody you never met?" asked Sol. "You've got to know your boss."

Sol had caught him completely off guard.

"You know what," continued Sol. "You get the time off work and I'll pay for a trip for you to Rome."

That's exactly what Sol Polk did.

When it came to promoting, there was none better than Sol. With every purchase of $25 or more, he would give away a case of apples from Washington state. During the holiday season, he would give away a free Christmas tree with every $25 purchase. He sure knew how to get people into the store.

Every year, about the first of December, my kids would ask me if Sol Polk's truck had arrived yet. Without fail, the big yellow Polk Bros. truck would pull up to the house in early December with Christmas gifts. One year it was a full size pool table, another year bicycles and sleighs. You name it, he brought it. Christmas trees, clothing, cases of apples and oranges. Hell, we were supplying the neighborhood.

Sol was so good and so generous. I never had a better friend.

When I started at Time Inc. in New York 1946, I was making $5,000 a year.

Two years later, I was transferred to Chicago to head up *Life International*. My salary was boosted to $7,000 with a minor expense account for travel. At *Life International*, we worked mostly with export managers of major corporations such as International Harvester and Allis-Chalmers. After the war, many of the smaller countries needed machinery and *Life International* was an excellent vehicle for corporations to display their products.

After I went to *Life* magazine, my salary rose to $10,000, but more importantly, I went on the executive payroll. That meant, I was paid once a month (instead of every two weeks) and was told to join both a city club and a country club of my choosing. I decided to join the Chicago Athletic Club and the North Shore Country Club. These were two of the finest clubs in the area and I made good use of them.

Time Inc. publisher Harry Luce was very civic minded and he thought it was important for his executives to belong to civic clubs, city clubs and country clubs. Time Inc. paid for these memberships. Incidentally, at the time the initiation fee at North Shore Country Club was $800. I shudder to think what it is today.

One of the perks of working at Time Inc. was receiving a membership at the exclusive North Shore Country Club in Glenview, a suburb of Chicago. While at the club, I became acquainted with a fine young caddy/starter named Don Barr. Don was also responsible for keeping the golf handicaps.

At that time, Chick Evans—who was very prominent in business and golf in the Chicago area—had initiated a scholarship program for deserving young caddies. Chick had been an outstanding golfer, having won the U.S. Open as an amateur in 1916. The Evans scholarship provided worthy young caddies with a full scholarship to college.

As a member of the greens committee at North Shore Country Club, I had the privilege of recommending outstanding young caddies for an Evans Scholarship. In 1952, I nominated Don Barr for this prestigious award. He was the first caddy I nominated. Don received a full scholarship to Notre Dame, beginning the following year.

Four years later, after obtaining his degree at South Bend, I received a phone call from Don.

"You got me to college, now can you get me a job?"

Well, I didn't have anything available at the time, so I directed Don towards Fred Love in production. Fred was able to get Don started at Time Inc. From there, Don rose like a meteor through the company. He was soon transferred to Paris and, before long, returned to New York to become publisher of *Sports Illustrated*. Currently, Donald Barr serves as executive vice-president of Time-Warner.

For Don, it's a long tee shot from lugging golf bags at North Shore Country Club. For me, it's a great sense of pride in being able to start someone like Don on the road to success.

One of the great characters at Time Inc. was Fred Love, the production manager for all printing in Chicago. A jovial fellow, Fred was always hustling, be it on the golf course or in the card room.

A colleague of ours, Ed King, the vice-president in charge of subscription fulfillment and circulation for all Time Inc. magazines, had passed away. Fred and I, along with our wives, drove together to the wake.

On the drive down, Fred said: "Too bad about Ed dying. I hate to see this happen."

I agreed: "I know what you mean. It's a sad event."

Fred had another thing in mind. "You know, he was

worth about $5,000 a year to me in cards. That's another loss in my book for this year. I hate to see him go."

When Fred joined North Shore Country Club, he informed the keeper of the handicaps that he was very comfortable with a ten handicap. And, indeed he was.

Fred had the swing of a caddie, but how he could play. He played just hard enough to win. Fred's annual matches with his brothers, Jim and George, were legendary. Fred always had me as his fore caddie. His instructions beforehand were simple, find his ball and make a casual effort on the others. On one occasion, Jim hit a ball in the rough. After a brief search, I found the ball.

Fred growled: "He already hit a provisional—just keep walking."

One of Fred's favorite golf partners was Frank Reilly, a plate maker in Chicago. Frank was a pretty good golfer in his own right, but the odds were too great when he played against Fred. If he were behind, Fred would always make up the deficit by contriving some kind of unusual bet on the last two holes.

Another of Fred's partners was Don Lytle, who was in charge of our chrome plating operation. Fred would call me and say: "Keep next Sunday open—I have Cupie ready."

Lytle was a short and plump fellow and Fred thought he resembled a Cupie doll. Fred had a name for everyone. He referred to another colleague as the Slob because of his eating habits.

I'm sure he had a name for me and I'm just as glad I never learned what it was.

Life was never dull in the company of Fred Love. He was one of the true characters at Time Inc.

Time Inc. occupied one floor of the La Salle-Wacker building at 228 North La Salle Street in Chicago. There were a number of other businesses in the building and it was here that I developed some special friendships, notably with Ray Kroc and Jesse Owens.

Jesse worked as a disc jockey for WCFL, a local radio station. He was a great speaker and a very good disc jockey. Also occupying an office in the building was Ray Kroc. At the time, he was selling mixers and styrofoam drinking cups. This was long before he thought of McDonald's.

One aspect of Ray's personality was immediately apparent. If he was for something, he was behind it 100 percent. But, if Ray wasn't behind an idea, a team of horses couldn't change his mind.

Years later, after Ray had made his fortune with McDonald's and had purchased the San Diego Padres baseball team, Ray and I renewed our friendship. I would visit him at his enclosed box at Jack Murphy Stadium in San Diego. He had many local visitors there. But, as soon as I arrived, he would announce in a booming voice:

"Jack, you knew me when I didn't have two nickels to rub together."

"That's right, Ray," I would say.

"Well, I've got a helluva lot of nickels to rub together now. Am I the same guy?"

I nodded in agreement. This little dialogue sure turned the heads of his new-found friends in the private box.

During my days in the Chicago office, I was often chosen to act on behalf of the Time Inc. executives in New York. If a situation had to be resolved or a political figure to be met, I was usually called upon to perform the task. The reason was that I was one of the very few people in Chicago who had worked in New York and the key executives there knew me.

When I was in New York, I had an office on the thirty-second floor, in amongst all the Time Inc. executives—vice-presidents Howard Black, Nick Wallace, C. D. Jackson and Dave Brumbaugh along with president Roy Larsen. In fact, I shared an office with Wallace. He spent a great deal of time on the road, so he invited me to move my things in there. How many vice-presidents would make that offer today?

When something had to be done outside of New York, they usually gave the task to me. They knew me. Naturally, this created a little animosity among my colleagues in Chicago who were often overlooked for such duties.

But, it was easier for New York to call on someone they knew in Chicago than to call someone out of the blue and ask them to do a corporate favor. This procedure was hardly unusual. It's a business principle that has existed for years.

As a result, I developed quite a base of contacts in and around Chicago. In fact, in those days, Murray Gart, editorial chief of the Chicago bureau, used to refer to me as "the mayor of Chicago." Still does, in fact.

In 1993, two friends from San Diego—Sol Price, the founder of Price Club, and Monsignor I. B. Eagen—were part of a contingent travelling to Israel. They would be flying over on Sol's private plane. When I asked Monsignor

With Senator
Charles Percy,
right, *of Illinois*

Eagen about the rest of the group, he mentioned that there was a fellow named Murray Gart from Time Inc. in the party. When I heard that, I told Monsignor Eagen to give my regards to Murray.

When they returned from Israel, I asked Monsignor Eagen if he had said hello to Murray Gart.

"Yes, I did," said Monsignor Eagen. "And, he told me to say hello to the mayor of Chicago."

5

Turning to Sports...Illustrated

When people think of *Sports Illustrated*, they think of the huge success the magazine has enjoyed over the years. And, for good reason. The magazine has become the most recognizable, most respected, and most widely read sports publication in the world. The magazine has become a vital messenger for followers of the world of sport. Readers wait with anticipation for the magazine's special issues—the baseball and football previews, the Sportsman of the Year issues and, of course, the swimsuit issue.

However, when *Sports Illustrated* began in 1954, it was hardly the success it is today. In fact, over the first three years, the magazine lost more than $30 million. There were grumblings throughout Time Inc. about this upstart sports magazine draining all the company's resources. The success of the other Time Inc. magazines such as *Life, Time,* and *Fortune* were keeping *Sports Illustrated* afloat.

I was asked to join the staff of *Sports Illustrated* in 1954 by Bill Holman, the advertising director. He made me a very attractive offer, but I declined. Harry Phillips, the former

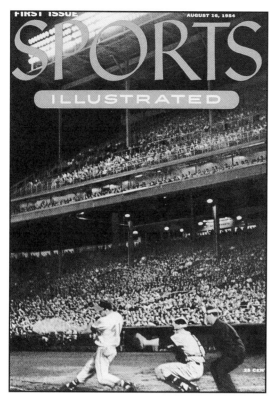

A new magazine is launched: the start of something big

advertising director of *Time*, had been named publisher of *Sports Illustrated*. Consequently, he hired many *Time* people to work on the new magazine. Having worked on *Life* for several years, I felt I would be out of place.

Phillips had great influence on Holman. He began to select people for the advertising staff. I couldn't understand their choice of Alex Colt from the Cleveland office to be New York manager. The most important advertising agencies were headquartered in New York and they needed a large presence there. *Sports Illustrated* needed the backing of these agencies and it needed it fast. Alex was a floor walker—I never saw him do anything but poke his head into offices and ask how it was going.

A former *Time* ad salesman in Chicago—Gary Becker—was made manager of the Chicago office of *Sports Illustrated*. An intelligent man, he had limited visibility in the Chicago market as most of his work contacts were outside of Chicago. I considered him a poor selection because he could not open doors in the Chicago market. The ability to open doors was essential because the advertising director would be hiring new sales people with little or no experience. There were no track records on which to sell.

Bill Curran, a mainstay in the Detroit office of *Life*, also joined *Sports Illustrated*. He was well liked and, although he never carried a rate card, he knew how to get business.

Sports Illustrated was truly a personal sale then—a believe me or trust me kind of sale. They had limited media research and marketing information at their disposal because they were so new on the market. Not surprisingly, media supervisors weren't going to take a chance on this fledgling publication without some cold, hard facts in front of them.

Gary Becker hired people with very little experience to staff the Chicago office. People like Don Hanrahan, a former basketball player from Loyola (Chicago), Tom Skinnell and Don Sperry had limited experience. Bill Kelly, a *Life* retail rep, and Bruce Marsh, formerly of Curtis publishing, rounded out the staff.

They were willing, but scared to death to make a cold call. On top of that, they weren't getting the support from their supervisor. The New York office believed that the way to secure advertising was to have a big party or take a bunch of account executives to the ball park. They didn't seem to understand the concept that advertising money had to be spent wisely.

Nevertheless, advertisers filled the first issue of *Sports Illustrated*. However, they weren't willing to commit to a schedule—they didn't have faith in the magazine. For them, it was a one-shot deal: "at least we're in the first issue."

I do want to emphasize that editorially—from the very first issue—Sports Illustrated was a darn good magazine. Sid James, the managing editor, was one of the best in the business. He brought in outstanding writers such as Tex Maule, Jeremiah Tax, Whitney Tower, and Jim Murray, to name a few. Murray, of course, has enjoyed a remarkable career in sports journalism, winning a Pulitzer Prize, no less.

Unfortunately, the market wasn't ready to embrace a publication of this nature. The time would soon come, however. With the expansion and development of television, it all changed. Madison Avenue soon discovered they could sell products to people in their living room while they were watching sports on TV.

At the same time, there was a sports explosion because of jet travel. Sports franchises were popping up all over the country. Teams could play on the East Coast one night and on the West Coast the next. Television and the jet airplane created a market for sports. Sid James was the first to recognize this development and he took full advantage. He had great vision.

Sports Illustrated soon became attractive to advertisers because it was the only major sports magazine on the market and it could back up what people saw on television. *Sports Illustrated* could give an event depth by chronicling the big games, the big fights in detail. *Sports Illustrated* was creating celebrities. As readers were finding out about their sports heroes, advertisers started to utilize these sports stars to pitch their products. And, look at the monster it has created. Many superstar athletes now earn more annually in endorsements than they do in their chosen sport.

When Jim Linen became president of Time Inc., his first priority was to turn around *Sports Illustrated*. Changes needed to be made in all aspects of the operation, with the chief focus on the advertising end. Consequently, Bill Holman was under extreme pressure to turn around the fortunes of the magazine.

Jim Linen asked me to meet with him one morning at the Blackstone Hotel barber shop in Chicago. At that meeting, he said he wanted Red Daugherty, Pete Hadden and myself to work on special assignment for him at *Sports Illustrated*. Red had been very successful at *Fortune* while Pete enjoyed similar success at *Time*. Pete was the brother of Brit Hadden, co–founder of Time Inc. Meanwhile, I was very content at *Life* in Chicago.

I told Jim that I couldn't do it. I liked my job and, besides, the General Electric account at *Life* was going great. He said I could stay at *Life* on the GE account and devote the rest of my time to *Sports Illustrated*. I could even keep my office on the *Life* floor while I worked for *Sports Illustrated*. I appreciated the offer from Jim but I was genuinely concerned how this special arrangement would be viewed by *Sports Illustrated* advertising managers like Gary Becker in Chicago and Steve Kelley in New York.

Jim replied: "I see no problem. You report directly to me."

I needed to get away to mull over the offer and its implications. I went to Miami Beach for a few days en route to a GE meeting in the Virgin Islands. When I returned to Chicago, I stayed on the GE account but started to make calls for *Sports Illustrated*.

It was difficult for me to go over Gary Becker's head. He must have known what was going on, but to his credit he never said a word about it.

Meanwhile, there was a meeting called in Chicago shortly afterwards. Bill Holman chaired the meeting. Morale was down and you got the feeling that something was about to explode. During the meeting, Becker's secretary delivered pay checks to the salespeople. Not a good move. Now everyone would know where the next person stood on the pay scale.

Those who did not receive pay checks were on the executive payroll. This meant they earned more but were only paid once a month. When a sales rep named Roger Thorson—who was not respected by his peers—did not receive a pay check, everyone knew his status. You could feel the tension building.

Bill Curran and I decided to excuse ourselves and go out for dinner. When we returned, we were greeted by an angry staff. Everyone had been at each other's throat while we were away and some incredible developments had taken place.

There had been drinking at the meeting and words were exchanged. Holman, backed by Kelley, had fired Becker on the spot in front of the entire staff. Everyone was worried about their job security. Tom Skinnell resigned on the spot once he had learned of his manager's fate.

When I heard the events surrounding Becker's firing, I was shocked. I called Howard Black in New York the next morning. He had already been apprised of the situation. I told him Becker should not have been fired under the circumstances. He agreed. Incidentally, Chuck Hanson, on hearing the details of the Becker firing, moved quickly to create an opening on *Life* magazine for Becker.

Bill Curran and I were asked to fly out to meet with the top executives of Time Inc. to discuss the matter. We were to meet with Harry Phillips, Bill Holman, Dick Neale, and Steve Kelley at the Greenwich Country Club. This was after an appointment with Howard Black at his New York office the previous morning. Howard advised me to be ready and tough. Meanwhile, Clay Buckhout, my supervisor at *Life*, told me he bet $100 that I wouldn't go over to *Sports Illustrated* permanently. I hated to be put in such a position.

At the Greenwich meeting, I was appointed Midwest manager at *Sports Illustrated*, which included Chicago,

Minneapolis and St. Louis. It was a plum job, but I really hated to leave the *Life* team headed by Clay. He was a wonderful boss, friend, and leader. I had the best of times at *Life*.

The staff I inherited at *Sports Illustrated* was young and inexperienced, but there were some promising individuals such as Don Sperry and Bill Kelly. Ironically, Holman had urged me to fire Sperry, but I resisted saying he was a good worker. I asked him to be patient. Sperry just recently retired from Time Inc. after more than 40 years of service. Bill Kelly, of course, advanced rapidly through the company and retired as publisher of *Money* magazine. Later on, a fellow named Bob Dillingham came aboard. He had been hired as a trainee in New York. We brought him out to Chicago and he did a terrific job. He knew how to work. Eventually Bob became Detroit manager and then was promoted to New York manager.

There were others, however, that didn't pan out. Roger Thorson dared me to fire him and I did. He thought that by getting in tight with Steve Kelley from the New York office, his job would be secure. Even after I gave him repeated warnings to pick up the pace, he challenged me and I fired him on the spot.

Another time, the New York office persuaded me to hire a salesman from Cleveland by the name of Jim Swan. He was less than productive and spent precious little time hustling business.

I found out what his priorities were when I took Swan to a sales meeting in Louisville. We had arranged a meeting

Another wacky promotion at Sports Illustrated. *Left to right: Dick Neale of* Sports Illustrated, *Stan 'the Man' Musial, Max Patkin, the clown prince of baseball, a guy named Leonard.*

for 9:30 the next morning. I was waiting for him in the lobby for several minutes. Finally, I decided to go up to his room to see what the delay was.

When I got there, he told me he couldn't meet me then because the tanning agent he was using hadn't dried yet. We needed hardworking, aggressive salespeople to turn the magazine around, not guys busy working on their tan.

Nevertheless, the market improved and we began to turn the corner at *Sports Illustrated*. By 1958, *Sports Illustrated* started to operate in the black. The fact that *Sports Illustrated* was still in business was a testimony to the vision of Time Inc. founder Harry Luce.

Any other executive would have pulled the plug on the magazine after all the money it lost in the first three years. But, that wasn't Harry's style. He hated to give up and he was determined to see the magazine turn its fortunes around.

Despite the great strides *Sports Illustrated* was making, I was still not as content as I had been at *Life* magazine. Quite simply, the spirit was not in me. My friends in the company began to notice my dissatisfaction.

Once I was golfing in Puerto Rico with Wes Pullen, and he could sense I wasn't happy. He asked me if I'd consider heading up the television operations at Time Inc. At that time, the company owned five television stations in the U.S. I told him it sounded like a great opportunity. He agreed to call me back the following Tuesday.

Tuesday came around and no word from Wes. By Thursday, I decided I'd better call him and find out what was going on. It turned out that Wes had flown home from Puerto Rico with Jim Linen and Charlie Stillman. Wes told Jim about offering me the job. Jim told him he had already offered the job to an ex-roommate of his from Williams College, Fritz Gilbert.

I was disappointed with the news. More changes were

made at *Sports Illustrated*. Bill Holman was fired and Art Murphy became publisher of the magazine. I felt bad for Bill. He had recently lost his wife in an auto accident and was under a great deal of stress. Fortunately, things worked out for him. After he left Time Inc., he went on to Yale Divinity School and became a minister. We still keep in touch.

When Pete Calloway became the new advertising director for *Sports Illustrated*, I knew my days were numbered. Previously, we had worked together at Bryant Paper Mill and we had our differences then.

Pete was always trying to snuggle up to the top brass at Time Inc. He was always the last to say goodbye to the boss at a company function. He made sure his face was front and center.

I also had an ongoing personality conflict with Steve Kelley, eastern manager of *Sports Illustrated*. Steve, in my mind, was an insecure fellow. My working on *Sports Illustrated* was a personal affront to him. He should have welcomed and accepted us—Red Daugherty, Pete Hadden, and myself—as people coming over to help. Instead, we were treated as adversaries. And management should have spelled out our roles to him. It would have made it easier. I told Jim Linen that Steve and I couldn't continue this feuding and that one of us would have to go. Jim never acted on my request. I imagine Jim felt the problem would just fade away. Needless to say, I was disappointed that Jim never addressed this matter. It was not long after that I left *Sports Illustrated* and returned to *Life*.

It just wasn't the same, however. My friends and colleagues such as Jack Morrissey, Chuck Hanson and Fred "Bud" Redpath had left for the main office in New York to work directly under Clay Buckhout. As a result, the atmosphere at the *Life* office in Chicago had changed dramatically.

I enjoyed my days at Time Inc. immensely, but I left because I felt I was betrayed while at *Sports Illustrated*. I left a good, secure position at *Life* to accept the offer at *Sports Illustrated*. The conditions upon which I accepted the job were that I would be backed on my decisions and that I would report to only one person—Jim Linen, the president of the company.

However, I learned one important lesson from this experience. That lesson was not to put a top executive in a compromising position. Having said that, I'm still proud that I stood by my principles.

In retrospect, the early days at *Sports Illustrated* were very stressful for many of the principals. The financial struggles took its toll on good people like Sid James, Harry Phillips, Bill Holman, Howard Black, and Dick Neale. After years of dedication to the company, Sid, Harry, Bill and Dick were summoned to work on this new publication.

But, to reiterate, America wasn't ready to accept a weekly sports publication, no matter how hard these individuals tried. Their previous successes on other Time Inc. publications would not ensure success at *Sports Illustrated*.

Unfortunately, these fine gentlemen were cast aside when the new magazine failed to live up to expectations.

(Ironically, Sid James was replaced as managing editor by Andre Laguerre. It was Sid who first brought Andre to the attention of Harry Luce. At the time, Sid was associate managing editor of *Life* and Andre was working in the Paris bureau. Sid was most impressed with Andre's contributions as a bureau chief and made it known to the top brass.)

It was ridiculous for these dedicated employees to be made scapegoats for the early failures of the magazine. When I see the current regime of the magazine taking bows for the success of *Sports Illustrated*, it disturbs me. They owe a great debt to those people who paved the way during the early, difficult years.

The brass at *Sports Illustrated* decided it would be a nice gesture to recognize former All-American players on the twenty-fifth anniversary of their being named to the All-American team. We would honor these players by presenting them with silver goal posts on the occasion on their silver anniversary.

In most cases, the presentation would take place during dinner in Chicago or whatever city was convenient. Surrounded by family and friends, we would present the former All-American with his silver goal posts—miniature, of course.

However, I decided to do something special for my good friend, Joe Stydahar. Joe was an All-American from West Virginia, in both football and basketball. In 1936, he was the first player drafted in the National Football League by the

Chicago Bears. Known as "Jumbo Joe," he starred as a two-way tackle (offense and defense) for the Bears. Later, he became the successful head coach of the Los Angeles Rams and then the Chicago Cardinals.

Joe and I were neighbors in Glencoe, Ill. and, having a lot of common interests, became close friends. When the time came to honor Joe—one of the most popular personalities in Chicago—I decided to make it a grand affair.

A luncheon was planned for Joe at the Chicago Athletic Club in July of 1961. We invited 150 people at attend, including such gridiron greats as George Halas (long-time coach and owner of the Chicago Bears), Sid Luckman (Hall of Fame quarterback for the Bears), Norm Van Brocklin (Hall of Fame quarterback for the Philadelphia Eagles and Los Angeles Rams), Marshall "Biggie" Goldberg (All-American halfback from the University of Pittsburgh) and Clint Frank (Heisman Trophy winner in 1938 from Yale). We also invited many other players who had played with or for Joe.

Clark Shaughnessy, former assistant coach of the Bears, was also invited. Clark and Joe had not been on speaking terms for some time, but I thought this would be the perfect opportunity to mend fences. (At the luncheon, before everyone sat down, I announced: "This luncheon can't start until Clark and Joe shake hands." They shook hands and the feud ended that afternoon.)

In addition, we invited some of the top business people in town and many of Joe's customers to this celebration. Joe was owner of Big Bear Container Company, manufacturers of cardboard boxes and containers.

Everything was falling into place just perfectly. All of Joe's friends, teammates and colleagues would be in attendance and it would be one great party. Nothing could dampen my enthusiasm as the big day approached. Or so I thought.

Sports Illustrated had a new advertising director in New York named Llewelleyn "Pete" Calloway. With a handle like that, no wonder he changed his name to Pete. Anyway, he had just been transferred over from *Fortune* magazine. Pete was an Ivy-League kind of guy who just rubbed me the wrong way. Well, on the morning of the luncheon, Pete arrived in town.

Pete asked me what I was doing for lunch. I tried to avoid the question, but finally blurted out the news that we were having a luncheon for Joe. I felt obliged to ask him to attend. Much to my chagrin, Pete accepted my invitation.

You see, I had this feeling that Pete was going to use this opportunity to make an advertising pitch for *Sports Illustrated* and that's the last thing I wanted. He'd get up and tell everyone how many women we were reaching and how many red-headed carpenters read the magazine. All morning, I'm thinking to myself: "this guy's going to ruin the luncheon."

When we arrive at the luncheon, Pete insists on sitting at the head table. Naturally, I had to introduce him. And, just as I feared, he feels compelled to make a speech. He starts talking about the cost of four-color pages, the value of four-color versus two-color and so on. The audience has no interest in what he's talking about and I'm gradually sinking in my seat.

We were there to toast Joe Stydahar and be among friends and Pete is up making his advertising pitch. Norm Van Brocklin is sitting next to me and he can tell I'm embarrassed by the situation. So, Norm takes out a marking pen and in large, bold letters, writes on the tablecloth: "This guy is full of shit!" At that moment, Pete looks down and completely loses his train of thought. Needless to say, he quickly wrapped up his speech. Fortunately, the rest of the afternoon was a huge success.

Jack with Bears' great Joe Stydahar at Wrigley Field

As I was driving home with Sid Luckman from the affair, he asked me about the guy who made the speech. I told him he was the new advertising director for the magazine.

Sid turned to me and made the following observation: "I can't predict things, but I don't think you guys are going to get along very well."

That was the understatement of the year. As a quarterback, Sid was pretty good at reading defenses. That day, I found out he was also pretty good at reading people.

When I first joined *Sports Illustrated*, I quickly discovered that the Chicago office was in a state of disarray. They didn't know the meaning of a full day's work and had suffered from a lack of leadership. The staff wasn't even aware of the magazine's desperate financial state. They just carried on as if everything was alright.

If it hadn't been for Harry Luce and his perseverance, *Sports Illustrated* wouldn't have made it. You don't lose $35 to $40 million dollars over the course of three years and remain operating. How long could the other publications afford to carry *Sports Illustrated*?

Nevertheless, it was apparent to me that both the New York and Chicago offices were living high off the hog despite the dire financial condition of the magazine. It seemed nobody was putting any pressure on them to get results. The magazine's content was good. It just hadn't caught on yet. Of course, over time the magazine became a great success.

One day, I overheard one of the secretaries in the Chicago office tell a caller on the phone that a particular salesman was in conference. I was stunned. As far as I'm concerned, if you're a salesman and you're in the office, you're never in conference. It's easier to say, "he's out of the office—he'll call you when he returns." To say that the salesman is in conference when a potential buyer is on the line is a horrible sin.

So, I went downstairs and made a call to the same secretary. I got the same, stock answer: "he's in conference."

I replied: "I'm a customer and I'd like you to get him out of conference or I'm not going to give you the order."

I still got the same response. Immediately, I returned to the office and conducted a brief meeting with the secretaries and the salespeople. No longer would callers be told that salespeople were in conference.

Nevertheless, we had some outstanding people in the office, such as Bill Kelly. Bill was a very good worker, but there was one problem. I noticed that he was leaving the office early every afternoon.

"How come you leave the office at 4 o'clock every day, Bill?" I asked. "I know you're not out making calls."

Bill grinned and replied: "It only took you two days to catch on. The other guy never caught on."

It turned out that Bill was leaving early so he could meet up with his buddies on the train for their daily gin rummy game. He explained that these games brought him an extra $60-$100 per month. I gave Bill an ultimatum.

"Bill, we're in bad shape," I said. "Either you give us 100

percent of your time or you give the train 100 percent of your time. Just don't split us up."

Fortunately, Bill changed his ways and devoted his full attention to the magazine. Subsequently, his career at Time Inc. flourished. He was later transferred to New York and when he retired he was publisher of *Money* magazine. I don't take credit for his success, but I was happy I was able to change his work habits.

My fascination with barber's chairs dates back to 1954 and a visit to the Jim Norris family estate on Long Island. At that time, the Norris family may have been the most powerful family in American sports. They owned New York's Madison Square Garden, the Boston Garden, Chicago Stadium and the Olympia in Detroit, four of the most hallowed sports arenas in the world.

Through my association with Tommy Ivan—the general manager of the Chicago Blackhawks hockey club—I was introduced to Jimmy Norris. The Norris family had built quite an empire in the sports world, particularly in boxing and hockey. They owned the four U.S.-based NHL teams (the Blackhawks, New York Rangers, Boston Bruins and Detroit Red Wings) and controlled the powerful International Boxing Club (IBC).

At that time, as is the case today, there had been much speculation as to the involvement of the mob in the sport of boxing. In one of its first issues, *Sports Illustrated* did an exposé on the IBC. The article was written by Sam Welles, a religion editor at *Life*. He knew nothing about boxing and nothing about sports, in general. But somehow, the editors at *Sports Illustrated* thought he would do a thorough job because of his superb writing and research skills.

Sam was told to contact me because I knew most of the key people in boxing. I was working at *Life* at the time. I told Sam that if he wanted to get the real lowdown on the fight game, he should see my friend Bill Daly in Paterson, N.J. Sam met with Bill and the story turned out great. However,

Tommy Ivan: The record shows one of the greatest hockey coaches and general managers of all time

the IBC did take some pretty good shots in the article.

The result was that *Sports Illustrated* was barred from all IBC events. What the magazine didn't realize was that the Norris family not only controlled the IBC, but also all the buildings in which IBC events were staged. All of which meant that *Sports Illustrated* was barred from hockey games, ice shows, track events, you name it.

Naturally, the executives at Time Inc. were very concerned. Vice-president Howard Black asked me to see if

Forty years later, I have my own barber's chair

I couldn't rectify the situation. After all, *Sports Illustrated* wouldn't be able to do its job very well if it didn't have access to these buildings and the events held within them. My job was to meet with Norris.

I used my connection with Tommy Ivan to set up an appointment with Norris. Tommy had to confer with Norris and I went along for the meeting at Norris' estate on Long Island. Fortunately, the problems between *Sports Illustrated* and the IBC were resolved during this meeting.

However, as far as I was concerned the most memorable moment from that visit occurred when Tommy and I arrived at the estate. Jimmy had a barber's chair sitting on the front porch and both Tommy and I were required to have a haircut.

Since 1954, I have been in the market to buy an old time barber's chair. In September 1993—nearly 40 years later—I finally purchased one of my own. A beautiful chair—circa 1910—proudly sits in the corner of my office today. A monument to Jimmy Norris.

At *Sports Illustrated*, the editors went that extra mile for our readers. In covering stories, they weren't afraid to take a risk, to try something out of the ordinary. To me, this is what separates a good magazine from a truly outstanding publication.

In preparing to cover the Sugar Ray Robinson-Gene Fullmer fight at the Chicago Stadium in 1957, our photo people decided to experiment. Instead of ringside level photo shots, they installed overhead cameras, right up there with the ring lights.

They wired each ring post, which would allow the photographers to sit at ringside and push a button to take the shot. However, unbeknownst to the photographers, someone had cut through the wires on each ring post, save one. However, that one aerial shot allowed us to get some of our best ring shots ever.

We decided to use our creativity in hockey as well. When the Chicago Blackhawks great left winger, Bobby Hull, was approaching fifty goals during the 1961-62 season, we decided to put the camera on the milestone goal. After he had reached forty-nine goals, we received permission from the National Hockey League to install a camera in both goal nets to catch the historic goal. Wherever Hull and the Blackhawks were playing, the camera would be on them. From Chicago to Detroit to New York and back to Chicago.

Finally, Hull scored number fifty in front of the hometown fans. It was a great night and I was there. The ovation lasted more than ten minutes and *Sports Illustrated* got the shot of the goal. To this day, I still think Hull's team-mate Eric Nesterenko tipped in the goal. When I questioned Nesterenko afterwards, all he did was smile and say they had to get the milestone behind them and get on with their remaining games.

There was something magical about Sunday night hockey games at Chicago Stadium. The attendance was always recorded as 16,666 (for fire regulations), but on many nights there were more than 20,000 in the stands. It was a wonderful atmosphere and my older boys (Jack and Michael) loved going to the games with me. The boys are all hockey fans and Mike played well enough to earn a scholarship to Providence College. He played one year of freshman and three years of varsity hockey at Providence.

To this day, I have many fond recollections of those Sunday nights at the Stadium.

One thing I found out quickly while at Time Inc. was the power and influence of professional athletes. Successful business people were in awe of sports figures and would do almost anything to meet them and associate with them.

I had met Fred Miller, the head of Miller Brewing Company, on many occasions while working at *Life*. I happened to know Fred was a big sports fan. It so happened that I was friendly with Tommy Henrich and George "Snuffy" Stirnweiss of the New York Yankees. The Yankees were in town to play the White Sox and, on an off-day, I asked Tommy and George to accompany me up to Milwaukee to meet Fred. During that meeting, the two players were given—at no charge—a Miller Hi-Life distributorship in New Brunswick, N.J.

After that successful meeting, I asked Tommy and George if they would mind if we stopped at another client, Allis-Chalmers in West Allis, Wis. I figured it was the least they could do, considering the sweet deal I had helped arrange.

At the time, Time Inc. was having trouble with Allis-Chalmers, which had been a major advertiser. The trouble stemmed from some editorials we had written on a labor disturbance at Allis-Chalmers. I had tried to see the president, Mr. Roberts, for some time and he had always brushed me off. But, he always said, "call me the next time you're in Milwaukee."

I had to figure out a way to see him, so I asked my friend, Joe Ryan, the assistant secretary treasurer at Allis-Chalmers, for some advice.

"He's a helluva baseball fan, Jack," said Joe. "He's nuts about the game."

With that in mind, I persuaded the ball players to make a call with me at Allis-Chalmers. We arrived unannounced and I called Mr. Roberts' office from the lobby phone. When I finally got through to him, he started to give me the brush off again, saying to call him next time I'm in town. Before he could hang up the phone, I interjected.

"But, the people who are with me won't be here next time."

"Who might that be?" he inquired.

"Tommy Henrich and George Stirnweiss."

"The ball players?"

When I said yes, he bolted down four flights of stairs to meet his heroes. We had a most congenial and productive meeting. Needless to say, our differences with Allis-Chalmers were resolved and business went well from that point on.

Sadly, George Stirnweiss was killed in a tragic train accident on September 15, 1958 at the age of 40. My colleague at Time Inc., Jim Ainslie, called me from New York with the terrible news.

George was known for his speed and this was one time where his speed worked against him. He lived in South Jersey and was on the train headed from Red Bank, N.J. to New York. George made the train by sprinting and catching the last car.

The train plunged into Newark Bay as the bridgeman neglected to close the railroad bridge going over to Newark Bay. There were no survivors. George, who had just retired from the major leagues, left a wife and six small children. At the time, George had been working with the *New York Journal American* in organizing youth baseball all-star games.

I was stunned when I received the news of George's death. I called my friend, Fred Lacey, who had just started his law practice in Newark. He called George's widow, Jane, and offered to look after the compensation suit with the railroad. The settlement for George's family was $250,000. Can you imagine what that would be today? Certainly it would have been well into the millions of dollars.

It was a tragic end to the life of a dear friend.

When *Sports Illustrated* was having a difficult time, I told the Allis-Chalmers story to Time Inc. vice-president Howard Black. We agreed that a magazine like *Sports Illustrated*

could use name athletes to its benefit. For example, if a company bought a certain number of ads in *Sports Illustrated*, we would guarantee having a name athlete at their next sales meeting.

Not only did Howard embrace the idea, but not long after, Dick Neale, the promotions director at *Sports Illustrated*, assigned a fellow named Keith Morris to the task of lining up athletes for such occasions. (Ironically, I had been doing the same thing with many personal friends such as Sid Luckman, Jesse Owens and Joe Stydahar—at no charge.)

Keith got himself a bundle of money to entice the athletes. They were paid anywhere from $50 to $1,500 per appearance. This was the forerunner of the use of celebrity athletes as we know it today.

At the same time, George Allen, who was the defensive backfield coach for the Chicago Bears, would call me every Monday morning to see if I had any speaking engagements for him. George, of course, went on to become the successful head coach of the Los Angeles Rams and the Washington Redskins. Anyway, I arranged for George to deliver a couple of speeches at $25 apiece.

But, George had a knack of cutting separate deals on his own for sponsor products and other perks. Once, he arranged to send his kids to an exclusive summer camp free of charge. He was a great self promoter. While in Washington, he had an open door to the White House and was appointed to the President's Council on Physical Fitness.

George Allen was well–known for squeezing everything out of a deal. Some of the deals he arranged while with the

Rams, Redskins and later with the Arizona Wranglers were legendary. In fact, Edward Bennett Williams, former owner of the Redskins, once said of Allen: "I gave him an unlimited expense account and he exceeded it."

A few years later, when I was working for Curtis Publishing, Page Thompson, the Chicago manager of *Ladies Home Journal*, came to me with a proposal. He knew I had arranged for athletes to make appearances on behalf of *Sports Illustrated* and he wanted to do likewise for *Ladies Home Journal*. Page suggested we recruit a couple members of the Chicago Bears. So, we hired Mike Ditka, the Bears' all-

Another Sports Illustrated *promotion with golfer Julius Boros,* left, *at North Shore Country Club*

pro tight end from Pittsburgh, and Joe Marconi, the Bears' fullback from West Virginia, and the promotion proved quite successful. We paid them $100 each plus lunch for three days. What a difference a few years makes! Just think what Michael Jordan commands for three days of promotional appearances today.

While I managed the Chicago office of *Sports Illustrated*, I had the opportunity to organize a number of unique events. I received plenty of requests from sports figures to arrange

A youthful Arnold Palmer, center, *strides the fairways at North Shore Country Club with* Sports Illustrated's *Bruce Marsh,* left, *and myself*

special events for them while they were in town and I did my best to accommodate them—without consulting the New York office.

In particular, I organized a number of golf outings, involving the top players on the PGA and LPGA tours. For example, whenever Arnold Palmer, Gary Player, Julius Boros and friends would be passing through Chicago, they would call me to see if I could arrange a little tournament. They had just played an event in Milwaukee and had a few days before the next tournament started.

So, I called up the North Shore Country Club and asked the manager, Don Noffs, and the head pro, Bill Ogden, for their assistance. We had no problem getting club members to round out the foursomes. They each kicked in some money and the pros played for the pot, with the winner taking home an extra $1,000.

We did the same for the LPGA players. Mickey Wright, the top player on the tour at the time, would call me to say the girls were getting cabin fever and were anxious to get out and play. So, once again we arranged for a winner-take-all tournament.

I was a hero with the players and it gave the magazine a good name. When I forwarded the entertainment expense report to New York, they would always ask if we had any advertisers out there.

"Hell no!" I replied. "We had a party!"

6

As the Sports World Turns

My introduction to high level college football came through my friend, Ed Ryan. He did the field announcing for Northwestern Wildcats' games. One year, Ed asked me to join him in the booth for the home games. I accepted the offer, enjoyed the experience immensely and spent 10 years in that capacity.

One of my duties was to find out the roster changes, injuries and, most importantly, the pronunciation of many of the visiting players. Believe me, there were difficult names in every lineup.

I met the visiting coaches down in the locker room and found them to be delightful and cooperative. The kindest and most accommodating coaches I met were Woody Hayes of Ohio State and Tommy Prothro of UCLA. That may come as a surprise to those who didn't know them personally, but I found Woody and Tommy to be very kind, learned gentlemen.

In 1955, Northwestern opened up against Miami of Ohio. Lou Saban coached Northwestern while Ara Parseghian was the coach of the opposition. (Incidentally, Miami of Ohio was regarded as the cradle of coaches because many big-name coaches got their start at this relatively small school). Anyway, Miami upset Northwestern in that season opener and as we were gathering up our equipment after the game, I casually said to my colleague, Ed Ryan:

"I think we just saw next year's coach for Northwestern — Ara Parseghian."

Turned out, I was correct.

Ara Parseghian put together a good program at Northwestern and recorded a major accomplishment by defeating Notre Dame in four consecutive years (1959 through 1962). Things haven't been the same at this Citadel of Learning since the Parseghian era. Not surprisingly, when Ara's contract expired in 1963, the Fighting Irish of Notre Dame were hot on his trail. However, the chase was not without a few glitches.

A press conference was scheduled at Notre Dame to announce the hiring of Ara Parseghian. I attended the event with Warren Brown of the *Chicago American*. We were all assembled in the press room waiting for the new coach to arrive. After a lengthy delay, Father Joyce sent a student to Ara's room at the Morris Inn to investigate.

When the student arrived at the hotel, the key was on the bed and Ara was nowhere to be found. There was no room for Ara. The press conference and the announcement would have to be postponed.

It turned out there was a clause in the contract that was not to Ara's satisfaction. I thought that it was the start and the end of an Ara. Fortunately for Notre Dame, this misunderstanding was resolved in a matter of days and Parseghian went on to enjoy a fabulous career at South Bend. Ara was happy, Notre Dame was happy and the followers of the Fighting Irish were happy. Funny things happen in sports — even at the college level.

Still with college sport, when I was at Curtis Publishing in the 1960's, *The Saturday Evening Post* thought it had a great scoop. The magazine had heard that Georgia coach and athletic director, Wally Butts, had provided Alabama coach, Paul "Bear" Bryant, with team secrets prior to the Bulldogs-Crimson Tide football game in 1962.

The Saturday Evening Post printed this shocking story and the magazine was subsequently sued. The key executives at Curtis Publishing weren't too concerned. They figured it was an open and shut case.

What they failed to realize was that the trial would be held in Atlanta and there was no way the South East Conference (SEC) was going to lose.

The hearings began with a pair of Philadelphia lawyers — hired by Curtis — pleading its case. These lawyers couldn't have been more formal if they had worn striped pants and cut away coats. Meanwhile, the legal team for Bryant and Butts consisted of ex-football players.

The Curtis lawyers presented their case solemnly while the coaches' lawyers did everything but tackle the jury foreman to prove their point. Not surprisingly, coverage of the trial in the local papers was extremely one-sided.

The verdict went in favor of the SEC and Bryant and Butts received large settlements. We found out that it's a tough league down there.

Like I said, funny things happen in sport.

I've been asked many times if I thought there had been fixes in sport. I've always replied in the affirmative.

Boxing is one sport where this question surfaces repeatedly. If I were asked to categorically name a fix in boxing, I would have to defer. But, if I were asked if I suspected a fix had occurred in the ring, I would say yes. Let me stress that this is only my personal opinion. I happened to witness this particular fight in person.

The date was September 17, 1952 and the site was Chicago Stadium. The event was the Chuck Davey-Rocky Graziano welterweight fight. Graziano, in my mind, gave less than a full effort. Consequently, the outcome—a 10-round decision in favor of Davey — left a strange taste in my mouth.

Chuck Davey went into the fight needing a name win and Graziano certainly had the name. This was going to be Rocky's last fight and one more win was not going to make or break him. That's my opinion.

Graziano could punch. There was no denying that. In the ninth round, Graziano hit Davey with a real good shot. However, there was no follow-up, just a waltz to the ropes. This was a clear sign to me that on this night things were not on the up and up.

Didn't I once say, funny things happen in sport.

Before I jump down from my soapbox, there's something else that has been gnawing at me for years. If betting is illegal, why do we have a line on the games?

It's certainly for the benefit of the bettor. Do we have to say the red team is favored by 10 points over the blue team? Why can't we just say the red team is favored over the blue team and leave it at that.

Like it or not, the world of sport is big, big business. And, like it or not, gambling will always be an integral part of the equation.

7

A Trip to the White House

"Say Jack, see if you can get me an audience with President Kennedy? I'll check in with you later in the day."

When I left Time Inc. to join Curtis Publishing as a vice-president for a brief spell in the early 1960s, the chairman of the board and president of the company was Joe Culligan. Joe did not have an easy task reviving the struggling company, of which *The Saturday Evening Post* was its main asset.

He called me in Chicago one day and asked me for a favor. He wanted to know if I could get him an audience with the President. The President of the United States no less—John Fitzgerald Kennedy. He wanted to have his picture taken with the President. I told him I'd see what I could do.

So, I called my friend Jimmy McShane, who was chief U.S. Marshall under Kennedy.

"Not an easy assignment, Jack," said Jimmy. "I'll try my best."

Within two hours, Jimmy called back. "How about next Tuesday morning? He'll be able to see the President then."

Joe Culligan and I flew to Washington on Monday night and we met with Jimmy the next morning. We went over to the White House and Joe was ushered into the Oval office. Pierre Salinger, the press secretary, had a chat with Joe and a little while later the President entered the room.

President Kennedy had been briefed about Joe by Pierre Salinger. He knew about Joe's business career and how he lost his eye in the war.

"Joe," said the President. "Benjamin Franklin was a Republican and it didn't help him with the *Post*—what are your plans?"

Joe Culligan's motive behind this meeting with the President was simple. He wanted to call on various heads of corporations and casually drop in the President's name during the course of the conversation. Such as "when I was with the President last week..." It was a great ice-breaker and sure to get the attention of these executives. Hopefully, it would help secure their advertising dollars.

I wish it would have been as easy to turn around the company as it had been to see the President.

Joe Culligan's master plan to turn around the fortunes of Curtis Publishing included the appointment of five, so-called marketing professionals—Jim White, a great Southern gentleman who was named publisher of *Holiday*; Jim Fuchs, a former Olympic shot put champion and a fine gentleman; John Veronis, an aggressive, intelligent fellow, who was put in charge of all publishing for Curtis; John Miles, former Detroit manager of *Sports Illustrated*, who was named executive vice-president; and myself.

We all knew we were facing an uphill battle in trying to resurrect Curtis and we all dedicated ourselves to achieving this goal. All of us, save one—John Miles. You see, John was a fine amateur golfer. And, it wasn't long until we discovered that the only place he worked up a sweat was on the golf course.

John set up an office in Chicago and an apartment at the Ambassador Hotel. He never made a sales call or held a meeting. But, he was always working on his golf game.

While John was in Chicago—he would later be transferred to Philadelphia as president of Curtis Circulation Company—I thought it would be a nice gesture to hold a dinner party to introduce John to the Curtis staff and some leading agency people. Apparently, John thought otherwise. The guest of honor did not show. Must have been at the driving range.

We're all familiar with the saying 'You can fool some of the people some of the time.' Well, in John's case, it was all the time! It's hard to believe respected, intelligent people can be taken in by people like John. Unfortunately, I've seen it happen on several occasions.

Incidentally, before John left Chicago, I took a peek at his expense account. It started on the first day of the month—lunch with Leo Burnett for $150. The second day was a lunch with Fairfax Cone, also for $150. These $150 lunches continued for the rest of the month. I would venture to say that John would not recognize Leo or Fax if they were alone on the same elevator. John sure pulled one over on the people at Curtis.

I don't know if I've ever heard a better stand-up salesman than Joe Culligan. He was a very polished speaker and he always left a positive impression with the audience.

He also utilized a clever tactic before he delivered a speech. Generally, the dinner at which Joe would speak was preceded by a cocktail party. During the party, he would politely excuse himself by saying, "I have to get a few thoughts together."

Joe would seek out a quiet place in the room, take out an envelope and jot down a few notes. These notes were usually the first few words of each lead paragraph of his talk—a speech which he had given at least a hundred times before. But, those in the room weren't aware of that.

Then, when Joe was called upon to give his speech, he would remove the envelope from his pocket in a grand gesture and place it on the podium. He would then proceed to give a rousing and inspiring talk.

One evening, Joe addressed a group of marketing people

in Chicago at the University Club. After the speech, Tony Cascino, a highly regarded marketing whiz for International Mineral Corporation based in Chicago, came up to me and was positively beaming.

"Jack, wasn't that a wonderful talk," said Tony. "You know, he wrote that talk at the cocktail party. I saw him sitting in the corner writing it."

I wasn't about to burst Tony's bubble. But, for the record, Joe Culligan could have given that speech in his sleep. The notes were just a prop, and a clever one at that.

When I decided to leave Time Inc., publishing no longer controlled the advertising industry. Television was taking the lion's share of advertising dollars. Despite this trend, I received numerous offers to join publishing companies.

I accepted a five-year contract as vice-president (western manager) of all publications for Curtis Publishing Company, the parent company of *The Saturday Evening Post*. They were in state of turmoil, changing executives almost on a daily basis.

Nevertheless, in spite of the company's shaky status, I felt it would be a great opportunity. I might add that I received a substantial pay hike from my previous salary at Time Inc.

One of the problems with Curtis was that the personnel was old and out of touch. They did not know how to adapt to changing times. Many changes had to be made.

Bill Benton, the head of Encyclopedia Britannica and the founder of Benton and Bowles, a leading international advertising agency, was the leading candidate to purchase Curtis Publishing. Newton Minow was destined to become the new chairman of Curtis and Eddie Miller, the former research director at Time Inc., was also going to become part of the new administration.

A board meeting was scheduled for Philadelphia. We all arrived at different times and by different modes of transportation. I took the train from New York, Newt flew in from Chicago and Eddie Miller drove down. I arrived before the others, only to learn that the meeting would have to be postponed because a board member had died that day.

As I was sitting in the anteroom waiting for the others to arrive, I couldn't help overhear a conversation among three older gentlemen, who weren't exactly whispering. On the agenda for the meeting was the decision to dismiss Joe Culligan as chairman and replace him with Newt Minow.

Said one elderly man to his friends: "It was bad enough we had a Catholic running the company, now we're going to have a Jew."

No wonder there's no more Curtis Publishing Company. As soon as Newt Minow and Eddie Miller arrived, I took them aside and told them what I had overheard. Newt and Eddie turned down the jobs.

If anybody could have saved Curtis, it was Newt. But, he was never given the opportunity. I soon tendered my resignation. Nothing else measured up to Time Inc. and I decided it was time to take early retirement.

While I had a guaranteed contract at Curtis, I just didn't have my heart in it. And, if you don't have your heart in your work, you might as well pack your bags.

Which is exactly what I did. I came home one day and told Marge to pack the bags 'cause we were headed to Arizona to start a new career. At the time, Jack was in the Navy and Mike was at Providence College. Tim was entering his senior year of high school and Kevin was still in grammar school.

There was just one minor problem. How would we break the news to Gram? Gram was Marge's mother and she had been living with us for fifteen years. I decided to tell her one Saturday morning over coffee. Her response was the same as always: "Why not. I'd love to see Arizona."

Our worries about Gram were over. We were headed west. And, as I would tell Marge: "This is no dress rehearsal. If you're going to take the stage, make sure you take a full stage and enjoy it!"

If someone were to come up to me and ask me what I did during all my years at Time Inc., I might be tempted to reply: "What didn't I do!"

Like me, I'm sure you've heard countless stories about the fellow who goes to work for a company and ends up staying there for the next forty years, working in the same job, in the same department all those years.

Believe me, my career at Time Inc. was anything but ordinary. I worked so many different jobs, in so many different areas that I myself, couldn't keep track. I was a rare breed, indeed.

I started at Time Inc. working for Harry Faeber in corporate production. This division, under the supervision of Charlie Stillman and Dave Brumbaugh, was responsible for almost everything that did not come under the editorial label.

Corporate production was responsible for the printing of the magazines, distribution, paper procurement—ink companies, all the heavy manufacturing of our printing equipment, contracts for building of presses and paper making machinery, you name it.

Investments were another area of responsibility for this division. Charlie Stillman once purchased land for producing pine wood for the manufacture of paper. He insisted on the stump rights and, sure enough, they found oil under the ground.

Working for corporate production certainly gave me a great diversity of jobs and responsibilities. We printed at a number of facilities, including Donnelly's in Chicago; Cuneo Eastern Press in Philadelphia; Pacific Press in Los Angeles; J.W. Clement in Buffalo (for color inserts); Jersey City Printing (for *Fortune* magazine); and Bryant Paper Mill in Kalamazoo (our own paper company).

We worked with all the major ink makers and paper suppliers and made tremendous use of the U.S. postal service. I worked in all of the above plants. It was difficult for my co–workers to comprehend how I could be working in so many different places.

The common and generally accepted practice was that once you served your apprenticeship—usually two years— you were assigned a position in the division to which you were most suited. In most cases, you stayed in that division for as long as you remained with the company.

When I moved to Chicago, I worked for *Life International, Life, Sports Illustrated* and then *Life* again. I was indeed fortunate to work in corporate production based out of New York and then to make the transition to sales and marketing in Chicago. I was one of the first to make that switch. As a result, I retained strong ties with personnel in both areas.

I'm certain my many contacts throughout the company led to my receiving a number of added responsibilities from various division managers. I did these jobs without extra compensation. However, I'm sure some of my colleagues were miffed at being overlooked for these duties.

In retrospect, I'm delighted I was not pigeonholed into a specific area of responsibility while I was at Time Inc. I was given the opportunity to learn all aspects of the business and I could not have been happier.

8

Step for Step with Jesse Owens

I wish everybody in America had the privilege of meeting Jesse Owens. He was that good a guy. I met Jesse while I was working at Time Inc. in Chicago. We worked in the same office tower—the LaSalle Wacker building.

We developed a strong friendship. I travelled with Jesse on many of his speaking engagements and we formed a business together when we both moved to Phoenix.

When people think of Jesse Owens, they immediately think of him capturing four gold medals at the 1936 Summer Olympic Games in Berlin, with Adolf Hitler in attendance. There was a myth that Hitler would not shake Jesse's hand after the 100 yard sprint. Well, Jesse said he never got near Hitler at the time. It was a story created by a good newspaperman who reckoned that Hitler refused to shake Jesse's hand because he was black and because he had defeated the Germans in the race.

Jesse told me it was the greatest story ever told because it kept his name in the forefront for a long time. Jesse never went out of his way to deny the story, but admitted that he never met Hitler.

Nevertheless, when we went on speaking tours around the country, Jesse began his talk with a story about Hitler. He would say: "No, I never met Hitler, never shook his hand, was never invited to shake his hand."

Then Jesse would relate a story about Hitler to the audience. Before the end of the war, Hitler felt that things were getting bad, so he went to visit an astrologer to ask him some questions about the future of Germany.

"Is Germany going to win or lose the war?" asked Hitler.

"Germany will lose the war," replied the astrologer.

"When Germany loses the war, will I lose my life?"

"Yes, you will lose your life."

"Can you tell me on what particular day I will die?"

"You will die on a Jewish holiday."

"On what particular Jewish holiday?" asked Hitler.

"The day you die will be a Jewish holiday," announced the astrologer.

I heard Jesse tell that story at least fifty times and it never failed to break up the audience.

When you travelled with Jesse Owens, you got used to being around crowds. People had a way of gravitating to Jesse. He was recognized wherever he went. If he were waiting to check into a hotel and someone noticed him in line, word would spread like wildfire.

Jesse never turned down an autograph request or refused to talk to someone. And, he never crossed the street to avoid people, either.

One time, Jesse and I went up to Alaska as guests of the

oilman's club. Les Gunderson, who had a place at Equestrian Manor in Scottsdale, was a friend of mine and he issued the invitation for Jesse to speak to the oilman's club.

On the flight to Fairbanks, the pilot of the Pan-Am flight announced that his favorite athlete—none other than Jesse Owens—was on the flight. Many passengers were already aware of Jesse's presence, but everyone stood up and gave him a standing ovation.

When we landed, Jesse had to sign autographs for everyone on the flight. It took about two hours before we could leave the airport. Incidentally, the same delay took place on the return flight when we stopped over in Seattle. It was a mob scene wherever he went.

We were in Alaska for ten days. We toured the area for a while, but it got to be boring. Then, we met up with Red Baucher, a friend of Les Gunderson's. Red was running for lieutenant governor and he managed to seize the moment. He would ask Jesse to meet him for breakfast. At those breakfasts, he would ask Jesse if he would mind speaking to this group and to that group later in the day. Jesse obliged until one day when we were in Anchorage.

Red said, "Jess, at noon today, we're going to speak to..."

Jesse interrupted: "Like hell, we're going to speak. I didn't come up here to go on a political tour. I came up here to speak to the oilman's convention and I think you've used enough of me. That's the end of my speaking engagements."

At the gatherings, Red would introduce Jesse, as "my good friend, Jesse Owens"—like he had known him for thirty years. In reality, he had known him about three days.

Nevertheless, Jesse was effective in getting people to vote for Red.

Jesse was a delight to be around and certainly one of the most generous individuals I've known. He always chatted with the porters at the airport and called everyone he didn't know "Champ." He also tipped them quite handsomely— usually $5 apiece. Finally, I asked him why he was so generous.

"Jack, if I don't give them $5, my name is gonna be all over Harlem tonight as a cheapskate."

I've often wondered how much an athlete like Jesse Owens would have made in today's world. When he was touring around the country, he was paid a retainer of about $25-30,000 a year by his sponsors and received about $2,000 per speech.

He never thought he was more important than the next guy. And, he never failed to honor a commitment. There would be times when he would be exhausted after travelling all day, but he would show up that night to talk to the local boys' club. If he said he would be there, he would be there.

His wife, Ruth, was a hero herself. She always stayed in the background and allowed Jesse all the attention. She preferred to stay away from the limelight and she raised three wonderful daughters. After Jesse's death in 1980, Ruth carried on with the Jesse Owens Foundation and all the other charitable work in which Jesse had been involved.

Jesse was unfairly criticized for not being radical enough and supportive enough of his race. These accusations angered him, but he responded to those charges in his usual way—as eloquently as could be.

"Look, you can't do it all in one day. I'm a paying member of the NAACP and I agree with all the things they stand for, but let's do it with controlled speed. Let's not do it by turning over trash cans and setting fires. Let's do it in a manly way. Not only will we get it done, but we will be respected for the way we do it."

He made these remarks at a predominantly black meeting—the day after he was accused of being an Uncle Tom. Believe me, that couldn't have been further from the truth. He was for the cause, but he expressed his sentiments the only way he knew how—in a dignified, effective manner.

When we lost Jesse Owens, we lost a great American hero.

When Jesse Owens had income tax problems, it created quite a national stir. As always, he handled these difficulties like a true champion.

"Your honor," said Jesse to the judge. "I was passed the baton and I dropped it."

For the next five years, Jesse worked at top speed to repay the entire obligation, with interest.

I was one of three people invited to testify on Jesse's behalf. The others were Ralph Metcalf, a star sprinter and Olympic champion in 1932 and later a distinguished congressman from Illinois, and Kenneth "Tug" Wilson, Big Ten Commissioner and former athletic director at Northwestern.

When I took the stand, I testified that Jesse made several appearances on behalf of *Sports Illustrated* and *Life* and would never take a penny, even though he was offered a fee for his services.

It was an ordeal that was, for lack of a better term, very taxing on Jesse. But, he handled the adversity as only he knew how, with style and class.

Spending so much time around Jesse Owens, I gained plenty of insight into the Olympic Games and the so-called amateurs versus professionals debate.

Jesse often said: "God gave me speed, but I didn't learn how to run until someone (coach Larry Snyder at Ohio State) taught me how to use that speed effectively. I only learned how to run at Ohio State. They accused the Russians of being professionals, but it cost a lot of money—maybe $25,000 a year—to teach me how to run while I was at Ohio State."

And, how he could run! Even when he wasn't feeling up to par. The date was May 25, 1935 and the event was the Big Ten championships at Ann Arbor, Mich. Jesse and his teammates drove to Ann Arbor from Columbus, Ohio. He sat in the rumble seat the entire trip and caught a cold in his back. He was in great discomfort when they arrived at the stadium. While his teammates went out to warm up on the track, Jesse headed straight for the training room. As he would tell me many years later, it was very doubtful that he would be able to compete that day.

Well, Jesse decided to compete after all. And, what a day he had! All he did was break five world records—in the sprints, hurdles and long jump—and equal a sixth in the space of forty-five minutes. It was, without question, the greatest individual performance in track and field history. An illustration of his total dominance that day occurred in the long jump. He jumped an incredible 26 feet, 8-1/4 inches to eclipse the existing record by six inches. It was his only jump of the meet, but it was a record that stood for twenty-five years.

Jesse was a great believer in the Olympic ideal. To him, it wasn't the medals that counted, rather it was the glory of the Games, the intermingling of nations. He always said competing was most important thing. He thought that there was far too much emphasis placed on winning.

During his speeches, Jesse would often pose the following question to the assembled group:

"Can anyone in the audience tell me who finished second to me in the 1936 Olympic Games 200-yard race?"

Without fail, nobody had the answer.

"Well, his name was Mack Robinson, brother of the great Jackie Robinson," continued Jesse. "Here I am talking to you while Mack is back in Los Angeles working for the school system. He wasn't that far behind me—probably a half a length of my shoe. We're making too much of this No. 1 thing. As far as I was concerned, the greatest thrill in the world is just making the Olympic team."

It's unfortunate that more people didn't share Jesse's ideals. We lose a basketball game to the Russians and we run out and form the Dream Team to ensure it never happens again. This obsession with winning at all costs is destroying the fabric of sport.

Sadly, the term 'amateur athlete' has gone by the wayside. The current state of 'amateur' athletics was clearly illustrated during the 1993 World Track and Field Championships. The winner of each event was awarded a brand new Mercedes. Nice prize, if you can get it. Or maybe not. As the winner of one of the events so succinctly put it: "If you're good enough like I am, you already have a Mercedes."

Jesse moved to Phoenix not long after I had relocated there. I owned a building on 7th Street and we renamed it the Jesse Owens building. A large neon sign marked the building. Predictably, it became a tourist attraction. People would pull up to the driveway, run inside and ask if it was the real Jesse Owens and if they could meet him. More often than not, Jesse would be the first to greet his admirers.

It was here where Jesse and I established a company called Champion Sales. We distributed jackets, sweaters and college uniforms. My eldest son, Jack, ran the company. Tim, my third son, also worked there.

Jesse was anything but a demanding taskmaster. He'd come in the office and announce: "It's too nice a day to be working. Let's play golf."

Who was going to take issue with him?

And, there was no disputing his generosity. Once, he said to Jack: "What are you driving that car for? You need a

Jesse Owens: Always the center of attention. Check out the tie on Jesse.

better car than that. Go over and buy yourself a new one."

Jesse Owens was a remarkable individual. And, he always gave more than he asked for.

9

Pleased to Make Your Acquaintance

One of the greatest characters I've ever met was Jimmy "Umbrella" McShane. He was a detective on the New York police force and was a great favorite of the Time Inc. staffers. I would run into Jimmy on my frequent business trips from Chicago to New York. Jimmy was a fixture in the diamond district and could be found in the vicinity of such popular establishments as Toots Shore and the 21 Club.

Jimmy McShane was the prototypical New Yorker—a real character. He was a former amateur boxer and he had the nose, scars, and build to prove it. He used to boast: "I had fifty-seven fights and lost all but one."

We became close friends in the late 1950s when he had been making regular trips to Chicago doing undercover work for the Kennedys. He was hired as a special investigator to monitor the activities of the Hoffa family and the unions.

The "Umbrella" moniker came about in 1954. Jimmy was a great friend of Rocky Marciano and he was present for the weigh-in before the Marciano-Ezzard Charles fight. The weigh-in was held at Yankee Stadium and *Life* magazine was there to cover it. The center page photospread that appeared in the next issue was a shot of Jimmy holding an umbrella over the champion's head.

The caption noted that one of New York City's finest was holding the umbrella. From then on, Jimmy was known as "Umbrella" McShane. Unfortunately, the police department was less than thrilled with the publicity the photo generated. They thought McShane should have been out chasing diamond thieves rather than at Yankee Stadium chumming with Marciano. Jimmy was soon assigned to the Bronx, but chose early retirement rather than accept the new assignment.

Nevertheless, Jimmy and I remained great friends. He also retained strong ties with the Kennedy family. When John Kennedy was nominated for the presidency, Jimmy became his personal bodyguard. On the day of the nomination, John and his brother, Bobby, were sequestered in a hotel room in Los Angeles while the press awaited outside, clambering for an interview.

Jimmy came out on the hotel balcony and announced to the press:

"The nominee will not meet with the press until one o'clock tomorrow."

At that press gathering was a *Life* writer named Hank Suydam. Hank yelled out to McShane: "Jimmy, Jack Leonard."

Jimmy looked down and pointed at him: "You come up here."

Hank Suydam and his photographer were quickly

The president-to-be and his brother mapping out strategy

ushered up to the room. A memorable photograph appeared in the July 25, 1960 issue of *Life*—one of John and Bobby Kennedy sitting on twin beds in the hotel room in deep conversation.

Hank Suydam, who tragically committed suicide a few years later, was so thrilled to get that picture. And, he always claimed that the reason he got it was because he knew me.

Meanwhile, Jimmy McShane later worked as the advance man for the Kennedy presidential campaign. He would go to a city a week before the nominee was to appear and would make all the arrangements for the rally, working closely with the local police departments. When Kennedy

Chief U.S. Marshall Jimmy McShane with attorney general Robert Kennedy and President Lyndon Johnson

became president, Jimmy was rewarded by being named chief marshall of the United States.

The spotlight always seemed to fall on Jimmy. When the first black student, James Howard Meredith, was finally admitted to the University of Mississippi in June of 1962, who was ushering him up the stairs of the school to register? None other than Jimmy McShane. There was great controversy and tension surrounding this event and, once again, Jimmy McShane was front and center. His mug was seen on every news clip that was broadcast that day.

When the attorney-general of the United States offers you his limousine for the night, how could you possibly turn it down? I couldn't.

Allow me to explain. I have known Ethel (Skakel) Kennedy for many years. My mother's cousin, Lil O'Connell was married to Bob Byrnes, a relative of the Skakel family. When Mr. and Mrs. Skakel were travelling, they would often call upon Lil and Bob to go up to Greenwich to look after the house and the children—all seven of them. They were only too happy to oblige. Every year, Lil and Bob would have a dinner for the Skakel girls. My sister and I were invited. It was here that I met Ethel Skakel.

I've stayed in touch with her ever since, even after she entered the limelight with her marriage to Robert Kennedy. One year I was visiting Washington, D.C. and I called Ethel at their home in McLean, Va., just outside the capital. She invited me over, but I declined saying I was on my way back to Chicago and just wanted to say hello before I left.

"You're going to Chicago?" she queried. "Why don't you go out and get on the four o'clock Eastern Airlines shuttle to New York. Bobby will be on it, along with Jimmy McShane and a couple other colleagues. Then you can proceed to Chicago."

When I got to the airport, I met up with Bobby and his group. Today, you would refer to it as his 'entourage.' Anyway, in those days, you pulled a ticket from the machine, got on the plane and they collected the fare at your seat. We all sat together on the flight to New York. I sat next to Bobby.

We were no more than 600 feet in the air, when the pilot comes on the loudspeaker to inform us that we had lost an engine and we would have to turn around. I said to the attorney-general: "We're going into the Potomac River and nobody will know I'm on the flight—the press will be all about Bobby Kennedy going into the Potomac."

We landed safely and had to wait for another flight. Consequently, we arrived in New York much later than expected. Bobby asked me if I was still going on to Chicago that night. I said it was too late and that I'd stay at the Dorsett Hotel overnight.

"I'm speaking at a police benevolent association dinner tonight," said Bobby. "Why don't you take the limo they have here for me down to your hotel and I'll ride over to the dinner in a squad car with one of the officers."

I accepted his offer, had a good night's sleep and returned to Chicago the next day. Now, how many politicians would give up their limo to a guy stranded in New York? Fortunately, I knew one who would.

Robert Kennedy was also a man of great compassion. Late in life, Lil O'Connell decided to visit Ireland to renew acquaintances with her family over there. This was after her husband had died. Unfortunately, while Lil was over in Ireland, she passed away.

You have no idea of the difficulties and red tape involved in having a loved one's body returned home until you have experienced it yourself. I can remember the delays and problems we encountered when my mother died in New York and we had to have the body brought back to New Jersey. It certainly adds to the stress level of an already difficult time. Naturally, the problems are magnified when a death in the family occurs in another country.

Fortunately, we had the attorney-general on our side. Bobby took time out from his busy schedule to make all the arrangements to have Lil's body flown back to America. It was done in a matter of days and we were all grateful to Bobby for his efforts. Without his help, it would have been a lengthy delay.

Funny how things work out in life. Some people that you help never forget. Others never remember. Pete Peterson falls into the latter category.

Bill Burchtold, one of the top executives at McCann-Erickson advertising in New York, once called me to ask a favor. He wanted to know if I could get tickets for the Sugar Ray Robinson-Jake LaMotta fight at the Chicago Stadium February 14, 1951. I said I could. I got tickets for Bill, myself and two other friends, Benny Stein and Sid Wells.

On the day of the fight, Bill called to ask if I could get another ticket for a new colleague in the research department at the Chicago office. His name was Peter G. Peterson. I said I could get another ticket but the newcomer would not be able to sit with us. That was fine with Bill.

It was a pleasant evening. We all went out for dinner,

enjoyed the fight (which was won by Robinson) and Bill Burchtold was glad we were able to include Pete.

Pete was soon asking me for tickets to any and every event that was happening in town. On Sundays, he'd call me for tickets to the Bears' game. I'd take him golfing at North Shore Country Club. I had become a great source for Pete and he took full advantage.

Pete was beginning to climb the corporate ladder. From McCann-Erickson, he went on to become president of Bell and Howell, then chairman of the board. Then, he began his political career.

Mr. Leonard goes to Washington: Harold Mayer left *and I flank the Secretary of Commerce, Pete Peterson.*

He was appointed secretary of commerce in the Nixon administration. We kept in touch and once he invited Harold Mayer and I to visit him in Washington. He told us beforehand, "you'll never see Washington better than being shown around by a cabinet minister."

Pete was right. We met everyone, including many people who became famous in the Watergate hearings. The president's office gave us a tie clasp and cuff links. It was quite an experience, even for a life-long Democrat.

Pete still maintained a residence in Chicago and attending Bears' football games at Wrigley Field on Sunday afternoons had become a ritual. I would drive Pete, Joe Stydahar, Sid Luckman and Clint Frank to the games. One day, we went to pick up Pete for the game and his wife, Sally, told us he was over at Senator Charles Percy's house having breakfast with the senator and President Nixon.

So, we stopped at the house to call on Pete. He came to the door and told us to wait a minute. After a few minutes, Joe Stydahar got fed up and said "let him walk—let's go."

When we arrived at Wrigley Field, Pete is sitting in the stands enjoying a hotdog and a Coke. I don't know how he beat us down there. Maybe he hijacked the presidential limo. But, this much was for certain: Pete would never miss a Bears' game, especially when he could get the tickets for free.

After his term in Washington, Pete returned to private life as chairman of Lehman Brothers. He spent ten years there and left with a comfortable multi-million dollar golden parachute.

Presumably, Pete has moved on to bigger and better things. Now, he flies to his home in the Hamptons in his six-passenger helicopter and maintains a magnificent apartment in Manhattan.

Pete doesn't have too much time for his old buddies. When you rub elbows with the big hitters, I guess it's easy to forget your friends, the ones who helped you on the way up the ladder.

This is not to say we have completely lost touch with each other. But, I think it would be easier to reach the Pope than it would be to reach Pete. It was not always this way.

Unfortunately, Pete Peterson wasn't alone in this kind of behavior. When I first joined *Sports Illustrated*, one of my salesmen, Bruce Marsh, asked me to make a call with him. We met with a fellow named Phil Howlett, who was working for McCann-Erickson in Chicago. I saw Phil several times after that meeting.

He made it clear that he was looking for a career change as he wasn't too enamored with the ad agency business. He indicated that he'd like to catch on with Time Inc., working on one of the publications. I told him I'd keep my eyes open. Phil would call me at least three times a week to see if anything had materialized.

One day, I was having lunch with Bud Redpath, the Chicago manager of *Life*. He told me that he was going to can one of his sales reps that Friday. When I got back to the office, I immediately called Phil Howlett and suggested he contact Bud and arrange an appointment for the following Monday. I figured the first one in would have the first opportunity at the job. When Phil told me he had set up an meeting with Redpath, I called Bud to thank him for seeing my friend.

Afterwards, Bud called me for further information on Phil. I gave him a glowing report. Phil was subsequently hired on *Life* in Chicago and I couldn't have been happier for him. He went on to enjoy a fine career at Time Inc.

Did I ever hear from Phil, extending a thank you my way, following this episode? Nope. Does this kind of treatment hurt? Absolutely.

A mere 'thank you' is all that's required. If anybody gives you a helping hand along the way, just acknowledge it. It never hurts to say thank you.

One of the most renowned photographers we had at *Life* was Margaret Bourke-White. She was a true professional and was willing to do whatever it took to get a great shot. She was one of the first women to make a live bombing raid and she managed to get some great war-time pictures.

Once she called to ask me for some help. She was on a Joseph Block steel barge on Lake Michigan. Margaret wanted to know if I could find a helicopter for her. She wanted to take aerial shots of a smoke stack at the Inland Steel Mills.

It was just after the war and helicopters were scarce. I wasn't sure where to go to obtain a private helicopter. Then, I remembered that Lewis College near Chicago had a helicopter school for pilots. I knew Bishop Shiel, one of the founders of the college. I called him and he was able to give me a contact at the school.

I arranged to rent a helicopter for Margaret and she managed to get all the aerial shots she needed. The story, which appeared in *Life* and *Fortune*, turned out to be great.

I called the school afterwards to thank them and I talked to the pilot and asked him about the experience. He said it was great but he couldn't get close enough to the top of the stack for her. He said that in his effort to satisfy her artistic and newsworthy demands, he burned his feet.

Margaret Bourke-White was typical of the skilled professionals at Time Inc. She was a great photographer and she knew how to get the best possible shot. Not only that, she was a real pioneer in a male-dominated industry.

All it takes is a brief encounter to appreciate the genius of a man. Take Leo Burnett, the advertising guru, for example. He was hailed throughout the industry for his creativity. I discovered he was also a wonderful problem solver.

When I worked at *Life*, one of our longest standing advertisers was the Hoover Company—the vacuum cleaning company. Leo Burnett handled the Hoover account from the time he moved to Chicago from Indianapolis.

One afternoon, I got a call from the New York office. The copy committee had determined that a Hoover ad—a four-page color spread to appear in *Life*—was not acceptable. They told me to go see the account supervisor.

The ad in question was for a 'beater' type of vacuum cleaner. The headline said: "Suction alone cannot get rug dirt out." We thought it was contrary to their other ads and, for that reason, wouldn't accept it.

I went to see Don Colvin, the account supervisor. I put the ad in front of him and told him we couldn't accept it as it now stood.

He looked up and told me in a gruff voice: "Go see the guy who wrote it—Leo Burnett!"

I met with Leo and told him why we were rejecting the ad. Leo was not fazed at all. He simply reached for a big red pencil from his desk drawer, drew an arrow in the headline copy and calmly inserted the word "all." The copy now read: "Suction alone cannot get all rug dirt out."

Leo proceeded to put an asterisk beside the line and then wrote a brief explanation below the headline outlining why beating the dirt out is better than sucking it out.

That subtle correction made all the difference in the world. It turned out to be one of Hoover's most effective ads.

Leo had transformed a poor ad into a great ad. It was easy for me to see why he became a giant in the advertising industry.

Over the fence or under the fence? That was the start of a lifelong friendship with Fred Lacey. Fred and I met at Northwestern midshipman's school in Chicago. We played softball against each other. Fred was the star pitcher on his team. I played shortstop for another team.

One game, I hit a ball to right field that I claimed went over the fence for a home run. Fred insisted the ball went through the right fielder's legs and rolled under the fence. "Over," I claimed. "Under," he argued. Neither of us would give an inch. This 'friendly' dispute persisted for years and years. Any time we saw each other—no matter what the occasion—the discussion invariably turned to that memorable play.

After that incident, we met on several occasions while in the service and became very good friends. We served together on the USS *Cythera*. Fred was an usher at my wedding in 1943 and I took pride introducing Fred to his wife, Mary.

My father called it the "sidewalk romance." The Leonard family and the Stoneham family had been close-knit for years. One night Fred and I had some time off the ship. My father said he would drive us back to the ship. Mr. Stoneham and his daughter, Mary, accompanied us on the drive. We stopped to pick up Fred and it was there that I introduced him to Mary Stoneham. They will soon be celebrating fifty years of marriage.

Fred attended law school at Cornell and graduated at the top of his class. Over the years, Fred has enjoyed an extremely successful legal career. He became famous as a prosecuting attorney in New Jersey and was responsible for running the mob from one side of New Jersey to the far end of New York.

Fred was appointed a federal judge by president Richard Nixon and took retirement from the bench at age 65 after 15 years. He was in great demand and has presided over prominent cases such as the labor movement hearings in 1991 and was chosen by then attorney-general William Barr to investigate the Banca Nazionale del Lavoro bank scandal in Italy.

It was such a great thrill to see Fred again at our fiftieth anniversary party in Chicago in the summer of 1993.

Fred and I have come a long way since that episode on the ball diamond. And, now, more than fifty years later, I can honestly say the ball went under the fence. But, the record shows—home run.

Like it or not, some sports have a hard time shaking a less than sparkling reputation. Boxing certainly falls into that category. To a lesser extent, pool or pocket billiards has been the victim of its somewhat shady past.

It takes a guy like Willie Mosconi to change one's image of a sport. When I started at *Sports Illustrated*, we had a promotion for advertisers to appear at the opening of shopping centers. We would invite some top flight athletes to drop by and give an exhibition.

Once, we set up a pool table and asked Willie Mosconi to give a demonstration. We struck up an immediate friendship. We often travelled together to these functions and stayed at the same hotel.

He would often say to me: "Do you think we ought to stay at this hotel with these young guys, or should we move to another place where we can get a good night's sleep?"

Willie was a terrific guy. He was a good family man, active in community affairs and just great to be around.

We used to discuss everything concerning his sport. I'd ask him about the prowess of Minnesota Fats and Willie would say he was just a hacker. About Jackie Gleason's talent with the cue, he would just shake his head.

Willie used to say: "I come from a sport that they say is the product of a misspent childhood. Well, it wasn't the case with me. I was given a good upbringing—my mother and father were great people. I just happened to be good at a sport (pool) and I just tried to make it better."

That he did. Willie died in September, 1993 at the age of 81. I'll miss his friendship.

I've been a long time admirer of Newton Minow. He was my next door neighbor in Glencoe, Ill. and we became great friends. A brilliant attorney, Newt may have been the only person that could have turned around the fortunes of Curtis Publishing. Newt had the intelligence, foresight, integrity and contacts to make it successful, but they never gave him the chance.

Newt was later honored by being named a trustee at Notre Dame. He was the first Jewish trustee at the university.

When Newt attended his first meeting at Notre Dame, he told me he made a personal request to Father Ted Hesburgh. He asked that they reschedule the football games from Saturday to Sunday and that they refer to the football as something other than "pigskin."

That was Newt. Always looking on the bright side and always with a quick quip.

I have never met a more astute individual than Newt Minow. He has the awareness and foresight that few people possess. As chairman of the Federal Communications Commission (FCC) under President Kennedy from 1961 to 1963, Newt made one of the more compelling speeches of his time. In 1961, his celebrated 'Vast Wasteland' speech triggered a national dialogue on the proper role of television in society, a debate that still rages to this day. It was the first time any chairman took television to task for abuse of the airwaves. He fought for public service television.

The FCC certainly could use someone with Newt's vision and wisdom today. I am alarmed with the current state of television. A recent illness forced me to spend a few days away from the office and home in bed. The quality of daytime programming appalled me. The lack of depth and intellect displayed on the airwaves today is shameful.

Why do all the networks have to follow the same script? It seems to me that those daytime talk shows focusing on such topics as 'sleeping with your best friend's wife' have gone too far. And, do we really need another prime time tabloid journalism show?

I don't think I'm alone in this kind of thinking. I wonder

if shows such as these would be on the air if someone like Newt were running the FCC today.

Through Newt Minow, I was introduced to Lester Crown and his wife, Renee. Although Les still resides in Chicago, he and I have been involved in a number of real estate ventures together in Arizona. I'm proud to say the majority of our deals have worked out very well.

Les, a very astute businessman, has placed great faith in my judgment. When I would tell him about a particular property that was available, the discussion would be simple and straightforward.

"What do you think Jack?" he would inquire.

"I wouldn't have brought it to you unless I thought it would go," I would respond.

"Then, go ahead with it," he would instruct.

I can recall three very successful deals in which Les never had the time to see the property himself. I bought the property, sold it, and sent Les his share of the profits.

Due to his numerous holdings and ventures, there are tremendous demands on Les Crown's time. As a result, I try to keep my phone calls to a minimum. One thing I admire about Les is that if you place a call to him, he'll return it. It may not be that day, but he will return it.

He learned business practices well from his father, Henry. I knew Henry for the last ten years of his life. He was a wonderful man, always cordial. Whenever he saw you in the waiting room at their office, he would come over and make sure you were comfortable.

Each year, I am allowed two invitations to the Senators' Cup tennis event at John Gardiner's Tennis Ranch in Scottsdale. Usually, Les Crown and Newt Minow are my guests. Newt hasn't been able to attend as many of these events as he'd like to because of business conflicts, but Les has managed to attend every event for about the past fifteen years. He thoroughly enjoys being part of the Senators' Cup and arranges his busy schedule around it.

Les and I have been working together for many years now and I hope it continues for many more.

His full name was Bruno dal Bianco, but to everyone who knew him he was affectionately called "Pino." Everyone loved Pino.

Pino was the popular caddie master at Skokie Country Club in Glencoe, IL, having worked there for an amazing fifty-five years. He was such a good-natured person that he became a favorite of club members, guests, and caddies alike. Pino was also a great influence on everyone who worked for him—an inspiration to all.

My sons Jack, Mike, and Tim all caddied at Skokie under Pino's tutelage. They adored him. I've often said that Pino helped raise the boys. He always had a kind word of advice or encouragement for the caddies.

When Tim was attending Northern Arizona University in Flagstaff—we had moved to Scottsdale by then—he would return to Chicago during the summer to work for

Pino. Thanks to Pino, Tim was provided with living quarters at the club. Needless to say, Tim worshipped Pino, as we all did.

When Mike and Cathy were married in the summer of 1970, we returned to Chicago for the wedding. At the time, I was putting a group together to purchase some property (Elliot Road) in Tempe. For all Pino had done for the family, I wanted to offer him a share—free of charge. No way, he said to the offer. But, he was quick to add that he would like to invest in the property.

"I have a few potatoes buried," said Pino. "So, when and where do I send the check."

When I offered to guarantee his investment, Pino shook his head. Pino would take the risk.

The property was a success and Pino did well on his investment. In fact, he became a regular investor in our ventures and, fortunately, did quite well.

Pino was a wonderful friend and a great role model for the boys. Sadly, Pino passed away in 1992. He will always be in our hearts.

My good friend, Danny O'Neil, was known as everybody's favorite tenor. He was legendary in Chicago and a personal favorite of Mayor Richard Daley. There wasn't an event held in Chicago presided over by the mayor that Danny wasn't the featured performer.

Not only was Danny a great singer, but when you asked him to sing, you didn't have to coax him. There were plenty

Membership at North Shore Country Club was one of the perks extended to Time Inc. executives. From left to right: Danny O'Neil, Harry McDonagh, me, Bill Curran

of amateur singers with good voices. Danny O'Neil was a professional with a great voice.

Whenever the Time Inc. executives came into Chicago from New York, they'd always ask me: "Do you think you could get Danny O'Neil to sing a song tonight?"

Danny always obliged. He sang for Time Inc. people in elevator shafts, the back seats of automobiles, you name it. He was only too happy to share his talent, and, more often than not, didn't charge for his services.

Danny's career started as a soloist for the Blue Jackets choir in the Navy. He sang with all the big bands and earned a great reputation in the business. In the early days of television, he shared a show with Mike Douglas out of Chicago and then became emcee for Merv Griffin's show out of New York.

I've always said that nobody, including Tony Bennett, sang "San Francisco" better than Danny O'Neil. When I think of true professionals, I immediately think of Danny O'Neil.

One of the greatest things about coming to La Jolla, Calif. was being able to develop a friendship with Buzzie Bavasi, one of the great names in baseball. His association with baseball started with the Brooklyn Dodgers.

He started in the lowest rung of the minor leagues and worked his way up to the big club. He became general manager of the Dodgers, then moved over to the California Angels in a similar capacity. When San Diego was awarded a National League franchise in 1969, Buzzie was brought in as team president. When he came to the Padres, he settled in La Jolla. He is certainly one of the most revered men in baseball. I've never heard anyone say a bad word about him which is the greatest compliment anyone could receive.

I had known Buzzie from my days at Time Inc. but once we moved to La Jolla in 1980, we became great friends. Buzzie and I talk on the phone every day and he visits my office frequently. We discuss baseball and sports in general. And, he never fails to humor me with another baseball anecdote.

It looks like Buzzie Bavasi is ready to make a move

One of my favorite stories is from his days with the Brooklyn Dodgers. He had just traded a popular Italian player to another team. The first call he received after the trade was announced was from his mother in Florida.

"I guess I'm next," she said. Then, she promptly hung up the phone.

Buzzie and I remained active in sport through our association with the San Diego Grays, an over-70 softball team. I joined the team in 1986 and played third base for the Grays until 1990. I retired after participating in the Senior World Series (70+ division) in Scottsdale in 1990. That year, our team

San Diego Grays—1990 Senior World Series runners-up. Back row, left to right: *Alberto "Chi Chi" Flores, John Donnelly, Ralph Lindenmeyer, Elwood Sager, Charles Strada, Bill Hogben, Tom McCarthy, Andy Rock, Van Vander Walle, John Bellock. Front row,* left to right: *Lou Guevara, Ray Skinner, Frank Russell, Vince Brynes, Jack Leonard, Sid Masters.*

reached the finals with a 5-0 record, only to lose the championship game to a squad from San Juan Capistrano.

Buzzie served as our director of player personnel. He was responsible for all player moves. He was just as shrewd as he was during his days with the Dodgers. He attended all the games and scouted the opposition.

When Buzzie first came aboard with the Grays, he realized the task might be more formidable than he expected. Observing the advanced years on our side, he was concerned about short-term memory loss. So, he quickly came up with a solution to this potential problem. When we took our positions in the field, we would have three pebbles in our pockets.

"After each out, discard a pebble," said Buzzie. "When you're out of pebbles, come on in."

That was Buzzie—always a step ahead of the opposition.

In 1986, Henry Antosz formed the Grays. Through my contacts at Wilson Sporting Goods in River Grove, Ill., I was able to arrange for uniforms. (It didn't hurt that Buzzie was one of our executives—he had been buying uniforms from Wilson for years.) Anyway, Wilson's Gene Dacosse, who supplied all the big league teams, provided us with twenty-five full uniforms. The uniforms were identical to the road uniforms of the Boston Red Sox. This was the big time. I'm sure the uniforms must have intimidated our opponents. Their outfits consisted of t-shirts and shorts.

At the very first meeting of the Grays, I had a most pleasant reunion. I spotted a gentleman in the crowd and asked him where he was from. He said he was from New Jersey. When I asked him to be more specific, he said Paterson. The fellow's name was Johnny Donnelly and it turned out we played against each other in high school. He played at Paterson Central and I played at St. Joseph's. Naturally, we reminisced and discovered we had many mutual friends. And, it seemed that whenever we met after that initial reunion, another name from the past would surface.

More than 50 years later, a reunion with John Donnelly from Paterson

I hadn't seen Johnny in fifty years and here we are in San Diego playing the infield—he played second base—for the same Senior softball team. It sure is a small world.

I truly enjoyed my association with the Grays. They were such a wonderful group of gentlemen. People like Johnny, left fielder Chi Chi Flores and shortstop Lou Guevara—just to mention a few—were a joy to be around.

We may not have won every game, but we had a lot of fun and we were certainly the best dressed.

"I didn't join the Navy to entertain at Sunday afternoon cocktail parties!"

Breakfast at Howard Johnson's in Miami was the last place in the world I expected to meet Eddy Duchin. I had been in the Navy for a few years then and had been assigned to the Submarine Chaser Training Center (SCTC) in Miami.

One morning, I was enjoying a leisurely breakfast with my friends from the SCTC, Clarke Kirby and Buzzie O'Keefe. We were talking about our days at the SCTC when the person in the next booth overheard us and asked if he could join us. He was none other than Eddy Duchin, perhaps the finest pianist of his day.

We had heard Eddy had joined the Navy, but we had no idea he had been assigned to the SCTC. It was his first assignment and he had plenty of questions for us veterans. He asked us about housing and we offered him a room in our apartment. He said he'd prefer a house with a piano. So, we set out to find him a place near us. We wouldn't miss the chance to be serenaded by this great artist.

Every night, without fail, Eddy would delight us with a concert, beginning with *"Tea for Two"* and *"Moon over Miami."* It certainly made our time in the service that much more enjoyable. In return, we helped Eddy with seamanship and Morse code.

When Eddy received his orders after completing his training, he was assigned duty in the Miami Naval Headquarters. He was livid. He joined the Navy to see some action, not sit at the piano. He went to Captain

McDaniel and demanded his orders be changed: "I did not join the Navy to entertain at Sunday afternoon cocktail parties!" said Eddy.

Eddy Duchin got his way. He went to sea and saw plenty of action. Meanwhile, I'll never forget those nightly concerts.

Incidentally, Eddy's son, Peter, has continued in his father's footsteps. He is known as the society band leader these days. How time flies! Peter Duchin was born while Eddy was in the Navy. Unfortunately, Eddy's wife died during childbirth and his in-laws in Long Island were forced to look after the baby. Eddy called them every night to see how the baby was doing.

I saw Eddy Duchin once after the war and it was strictly by coincidence. At Time Inc., I was assigned to escort Nick Wallace around whenever he came to town. I loved it. I got to go to the best restaurants, the best hotels in town.

One evening when Nick was in New York we walked over to the Waldorf Astoria. The first person I saw as I entered the hotel was Eddy Duchin, who was taking a break from playing at the hotel's Moulin Rouge room. We were so delighted to see each other. Eddy suggested we stay for dinner. It was too rich for my blood but Nick had a large expense account and who was I to argue. Eddy joined us after each break and we all had a terrific evening.

Another memorable evening in the company of Nick Wallace occurred after we had returned to New York from an exhausting day at Cuneo Press in Philadelphia.

Nick wanted to have his suit pressed, so he called the hotel valet. I was in the other room. When the valet came to the door to pick up the suit, I answered the door.

I opened the door and I was stunned. The valet was my cousin Dennis Gallagher from Tubbercurry, Ireland. I had not seen him since I visited Ireland as a 12-year-old. We had a grand reunion.

Nick Wallace was flabbergasted. "What the hell goes on, Leonard? You have cousins all over the place!"

10

A New Place, A New Career

It is true what they say—it never is too late to start a new career. The thought of entering the real estate and land development business had never crossed my mind. Having worked in publishing for so long, I had never given much thought to any other line of work.

After we moved to Arizona, I was hired as director of the new Convention Center in Phoenix. The center wasn't even built at the time, but all the hotels in town were maneuvering to garner their share of business. It was becoming a vicious battleground. The hotels were only concerned with their own well being and couldn't care less what happened with the Convention Center. It was not a pleasant situation and I left my position after a brief stay—too political.

Nevertheless, we were happy in Arizona and I was in no hurry to jump into another venture. As often happens, the most innocent of situations turn into tremendous opportunities. One day, our friends Harold and June Mayer came to visit us from Palm Springs. Harold—of the famous Oscar Mayer family—and I had known each other for many years in Chicago. While June and Marge were in the house, Harold casually asked me to keep my eye open for real estate property in the area. He had heard there were some good opportunities in Arizona.

Harold had certainly piqued my interest. I went to the Valley National Bank trust department and made some inquiries on property. Bud Meyer, a former FBI agent now working for the Valley National Bank, introduced me to the trust officer. Bud and I had mutual friends—Bill and Floy Quinn of Minneapolis. It turned out they had some vacant land in their trust department.

One property in Tempe intrigued me. I had heard Tempe, a university town, was a growing area. There were 320 acres on the property and the asking price was $2,000 an acre. I called Harold and he said let's do it. In May 1968, we struck a deal. Harold agreed to purchase 160 acres and I put together twenty-four other partners to purchase the other fifty percent. Seven years later, we sold the property to Dayton-Hudson for more than $10,000 an acre. For the small investment my partners and I had made, we were rewarded handsomely. As was Harold.

For the next ten years, everything we touched in the real estate business turned a profit. Ironically, I had become involved in a business venture that I didn't know a lot about, but I seemed to have a knack for finding good locations. My motto was the property had to be in a progressive area and on the road to something—not a dead end. I purchased mostly corner areas.

As a sidelight to this initial transaction, a gentleman

named Frank Knell expressed interest in purchasing the property before Dayton-Hudson entered the picture. I bumped into him at the Los Angeles airport one day and he asked me how much the property was going for. When I told him the purchase price was $4,000 an acre, he said I was out of my mind.

Funny how things work out. Dayton-Hudson had plans to develop the property into a shopping mall. But, when those plans fell through, they put the property back on the market. The purchaser was none other than Frank Knell. He paid $38,000 an acre. I couldn't resist calling him on the phone once I heard the news.

"Hey, Frank," I said. "Who's out of their mind now!"

A kingdom for your horse; a castle for you.

A catchy slogan, but a business venture that failed miserably. That's the way we advertised Equestrian Manor, the property I purchased along with Harold and Alan Mayer.

In 1969, I saw this great vacant property in north Scottsdale. The property, owned by the Robert Aste Estate, was on Cactus Road and consisted of 140 acres.

Bob Aste, a well-liked New Yorker and his wife, Peggy, a Southern belle from New Orleans, had settled in Scottsdale and had reached high society status in the area. Bob had a great interest in Arabian horses and had purchased this land for his prize winning Arabians. The only structure on the land was a very spacious, well-equipped barn.

After Bob Aste's death, Peggy decided to put the property up for sale as she was no longer interested in breeding Arabian horses. She compiled two lists: the first list included those parties to whom she would consider selling, and the second list—a much longer one—included names of parties she would not sell to under any condition.

I went to visit Peggy and told her that the Mayer brothers and I would indeed be interested. We immediately went to the top of her potential buyers list. Soon afterwards, we purchased the land—140 acres of prime land in Scottsdale—for $400,000.

Equestrian Manor: A kingdom for your horse . . .

All we had to do was resell the land and make a tidy profit. But, sadly, we couldn't leave well enough alone.

This was going to be our dream. We would be developers. We would have our own monument. We did it that way and we lost.

Some time later, Pete Peterson, who by now was running Lehman Brothers in New York, joined us as a partner and invested $150,000. When he came in, we were well into the building stage. The infrastructure was in place and there were now many homes on site.

. . . a castle for you

I had the first home on Equestrian Ranch. Harold Mayer purchased two lots, but did not build. His brother, Alan, purchased a lot but decided to live at another location in the valley. Meanwhile, Pete Peterson did not purchase a lot and did not contribute anything other than his initial investment in the operation. It was Harold and I all the way.

By the time we sold to Tom Chauncey in 1973, we had sold twenty-one lots, with fifteen home sites occupied. There were ninety lots on the property. Needless to say, plenty of blood, sweat, and tears went into this project. I planted or helped plant every bush and every tree on the site. Since I lived on the premises during development, I had to be available to answer all questions, sales calls, and complaints. I was on the firing line constantly. It was four years of hard work and, ultimately, great disappointment.

I was able to get feature articles on the property placed in magazines, such as *Fortune* and *Classic*, but the housing market in Arizona in the early 1970s was slumping.

Harold Mayer's legal and financial advisors recommended that for tax reasons it would be a good time to sell. He could use the loss. So, we sold to Tom Chauncey for $1,000,000 after having spent about $3,000,000 in developing the property.

To describe in full the details of this sale would require a book in itself. Suffice to say, Equestrian Manor was a major setback. Life certainly can be a humbling experience. After a spill such as this, I learned that you just have to get back in the saddle and continue on the journey.

In organizing Equestrian Manor, we hired the prestigious Phoenix law firm of Jennings, Strouss & Salmon. Price Waterhouse was also brought aboard to look after our accounting. We made sure we were surrounded by the best.

Our lead attorney was T. Patrick Flood, an outstanding individual and a former scholar/athlete. Patrick played freshman football at Notre Dame, before transferring to the Naval Academy, where he excelled as a midshipman and athlete. These days Patrick also keeps law and order on the football field as he officiates PAC-10 football games. We certainly utilized all of Pat's talents during those hectic days at Equestrian Manor.

We also formed a construction firm — M & L Properties (Mayer and Leonard) — to handle all of the construction and home building projects. We went all out.

We decided to apply for a loan at the main branch of the Valley National Bank. Our banker and loan officer was Roger Jensen. From past experience, I knew that the bank would demand documentation and I came to the meeting well prepared.

When Roger Jensen asked Harold Mayer for his credentials, Harold calmly said that he didn't usually make that information available. Then, Harold picked up a small note pad and wrote down his name, assets, and liabilities. He signed the paper, dated it and handed it to the banker.

Jensen examined the document, looked up and said: "This will fly."

We had everything in line but the market. Needless to say, I would receive numerous calls from Roger Jensen inquiring as to the state of my health. Roger would sometimes leave a message at Harold's office in Chicago as well. Harold would call me to ask if I knew what Jensen wanted. I think it's money, I told Harold. I think Harold knew that as well.

Despite the difficulties and stress associated with this project, there were still some lighter moments at Equestrian Manor. When Dr. Michael DeGrazia purchased a home in the community, he decided he should also acquire a horse in keeping with the equestrian theme. But, not just any horse. Michael wanted a first-rate, Arabian mare.

We did not have a horse of that caliber at the Manor, but I knew my friend Tom Chauncey — a prominent businessman in Arizona — had one at his ranch. So, off we went to Chauncey's. Tom showed off one of his prized Arabian mares and Dr. and Mrs. DeGrazia were immediately taken. They settled on a price — $20,000 — and a deal was struck.

"I would like to pay in cash," said Michael.

"Fine with me," replied Tom.

If you've ever seen $20,000 in one-hundred dollar bills, it makes quite a package. Tom stuffed the money in every available pocket he had. Surely, he must have slept with one eye open.

The saga continued the next morning. Tom's bank did not open until 9:00 a.m. and he had a prior engagement at 8:00 — an appointment with his barber. Tom arrived at the shop on time and loaded. More precisely, the pockets of his sports coat were loaded. The temperature that morning must have been 100 degrees in the shade and there's Tom sitting in the chair wearing his coat under the barber's apron.

The barber keeps saying: "You're sweating, Tom. Let me hang up your jacket."

"No, no, I'm fine," insists Tom. "In fact, I'm having chills. I must be catching a cold."

Must have been the 24-minute flu. Needless to say, the chills subsided once Chauncey got out of the chair and high-tailed it to the bank to make his deposit.

The Arabian mare sold by Chauncey actually belonged to P.K. (Phil) Wrigley, Tom's father-in-law. Tom later told me that when he informed Wrigley of the sale, it was the first and only time they exchanged smiles.

Equestrian Manor may have been a financial disaster, but it certainly introduced me to many wonderful people. People like Doug and June Willey.

After *Fortune* magazine had run a nice article and photo spread on Equestrian Manor, I received a message to call a number in Birmingham, AL.

I was not familiar with anyone from the area, but I made the call anyway. I told the girl on the other end that the only info I had was the number. She said I had reached the office of Mr. Doug Willey and that he was the proprietor of a General Motors dealership in Birmingham.

The secretary had no idea why Mr. Willey had called, but she did say there was a recent issue of *Fortune* magazine on his desk, with a paper clip on the page featuring Equestrian Manor. My ears immediately perked up and I left word for Mr. Willey to call me at any time, any day.

Shortly afterwards, Doug Willey returned my call and requested further information on the development. Before long, Doug and June Willey purchased a lot at Equestrian Manor, built a beautiful home and became our close neighbors and friends. A wonderful friendship developed.

The Willeys became great additions to Equestrian Manor and to the Phoenix/Scottsdale community as a whole. Doug was involved in many community affairs, even though his busy schedule allowed him limited time in Arizona.

Doug and June were just part of the fine community at Equestrian Manor. People like Dr. and Mrs. John McLoone, John and Marjorie Hagan, E. Tom Meyer, Dr. and Mrs. Michael DeGrazia, Heinie and Barbara Foss and the Gundersons from Alaska all became great members of the community. Unfortunately, we lost a good friend when Doug Willey passed away at a young age.

There's a silver lining in every cloud. Equestrian Manor may have flopped financially, but it was an unqualified success in terms of the quality people it attracted.

I met John Gardiner in Scottsdale. I knew his name and reputation for operating a first rate tennis camp for children and resort for corporate executives in Carmel, Calif.

There was a small tennis club on Camelback Mountain in Scottsdale that was never able to get off the ground. Despite having an ideal location, the club was always struggling. Finally, the club was auctioned off and sold for $275,000.

The new owners didn't know what to do with the tennis facility. Then, someone suggested they call in John Gardiner as a consultant. John came in, saw the location and the potential of the place and decided to purchase eighty-five percent of the property. The club was renamed John Gardiner's Tennis Ranch.

John hired an architect to design some forty-one casitas and he landscaped the area beautifully. At the start it looked a bit like an Indian village. But, after John took over, tremendous improvements were made. The casitas were

John Gardiner—one of America's great hosts

sold to individuals, starting at $50,000, with a $6,000 allowance for furniture.

Being aware of my Chicago roots, John said to me one day: "You have some friends who like to play tennis and you know some people in Chicago, why don't you give them a call?"

I immediately called Harold Mayer, who was already aware of the property. He had heard about it from Phil Frye, a co-owner of the Chicago Bulls with Harold and Eddie Higgins. Eventually, all three bought casitas at John Gardiner's.

Membership at the resort grew rapidly. It became a who's who of American business. Soon it became apparent that John needed to establish a homeowner's association. Even though I never owned a casita, I was close to the operation and knew many of the owners. Consequently, I was nominated to be president of the homeowners' association and I spent thirteen years in that role. It was a lot of fun.

John Gardiner was an outstanding operator. His very presence attracted prominent people to the area. Leaders in business, sports, and entertainment flocked to the resort.

In 1975, John established a unique tennis weekend/charity event called the Senators' Cup. He invited some forty U.S. Senators—Republicans and Democrats—along with many business leaders to participate in this event. It was billed as a friendly competition between the two parties. Proceeds from the event benefitted the Hospice of the Valley, an organization that provides home care for terminally ill patients. John's first wife, Barbara, was stricken with cancer and this charity was very dear to him.

The Senators' Cup is still going strong today and it has become a great social event for the political and business leaders of America. John Gardiner's charm and reputation has attracted such prominent individuals as Treasury Secretary Lloyd Bentsen, Senators John Warner (Virginia), Sam Nunn (Georgia) and Ernest Hollings (South Carolina), along with industry leaders like Frank Biondi (Viacom), Henry Block (H&R Block), Bob Castellini (The Castellini Company), and Robert Galvin (Motorola) to this wonderful event.

The Senators' Cup has grown each and every year and has raised some $3 million for the Hospice of the Valley. The success and longevity of this event is a tribute to the host

Art Buchwald, center, *holding court at the Senators' Cup*

himself, John Gardiner.

One year, Marge and I were having dinner with Senator Howard Metzenbaum (Ohio) and his wife, Shirley. Motioning to another table, Senator Metzenbaum said: "Talk about power. You see those three people at the table over there. They could blow up the world."

Seated at the next table were the president of Rockwell Industries, the chairman of Dow Chemical and a vice-president of General Dynamics.

A gala event, featuring Hollywood celebrities, rounds out the weekend's festivities. Merv Griffin, a friend of John's, is responsible for lining up many of the guests to attend and perform at the gala. A senator or celebrity is present at each table.

Alan King was the featured entertainer one year. He had been performing in Sun City the night before. That day, there was a violent rainstorm that created numerous traffic problems. Alan's driver was forced to bring him to the event via Bell Road, a route characterized by dips and valleys. The wash nearly wiped out the road that day. Leave it to Alan to find some humor in that ordeal.

"It was an adventurous trip coming from Sun City to Scottsdale. I knew we were in trouble when I saw a little Jew out there lining up the animals two by two."

One of the more popular 'amateur' entertainers at the Senators' Cup tennis tournament is Dr. Robert Albo. By day, he is one of the country's leading orthopedic surgeons.

In his limited leisure time, he is a multi-talented magician. You might say he's a magician with or without a scalpel.

Bob may well hold the record for most championship rings. As team doctor for the Oakland A's baseball club, Oakland (now Los Angeles) Raiders football club, and Golden State Warriors basketball club, he recorded a rare trifecta. All three teams won championships in the mid-1970s.

Bob and his wife, Marge, have owned a casita at John Gardiner's Tennis Ranch in Scottsdale for many years. Every year, Bob entertains at the Senators' Cup and, without fail, it seems there is always a medical emergency that requires his services. The cry of "Paging, Dr. Albo" is just as common as "Game, set, and match" at the Senators' Cup.

For guests at the Senators' Cup, it's reassuring to know there is a doctor like Bob in the house. One year, my wife, Marge, broke her foot at the event. Dr. Albo was quickly summoned from his dinner and came to her aid. Another guest, Tom Chauncey, provided his private plane to whisk us back to San Diego where Marge had her foot put in a cast. Talk about the royal treatment!

As a rule, Marge hates to fly. However, afterwards, she admitted she could get used to jetting from place to place in a private plane.

It's nice to have good friends.

I have known Bil Keane, the superb cartoonist, for many years. His popular Family Circus cartoon is syndicated in

more than 1,400 newspapers and never fails to extract a smile from me.

Bil is also in great demand as a master of ceremonies and loves to perform when his hectic schedule permits.

For the past nineteen years, Bil has served as official referee for the Senators' Cup tennis tournament. Needless to say, Bil's quips when the senators and celebrities are on the court far exceed the quality of play.

Each year at the tournament, Bil produces a work of art which is auctioned off at a special party. His work is often the highlight of the evening and usually brings in the top bid of the auction. All proceeds from the auction benefit the event's charity—The Hospice of the Valley.

Over the years, Bil has generously sent my family and I many wonderful cartoons, which proudly adorn the walls of my house and office.

I'll never forget one night in which Bil presided over a dinner honoring Father Michael Weischaar, a beloved Franciscan priest in the Phoenix-Scottsdale area.

Bil started his introduction by describing Father Michael as a pillar of the community, a man worthy of great respect.

Then he continued: "You know, Father Mike reminds me of St. Paul...the dullest city I have ever visited!"

Not true, of course, but a great remark, nonetheless.

Of all the athletes I've met, Australian tennis star Ken Rosewall stood right at the top. He encompassed all the qualities you look for a role model—ability, humility and genuine thoughtfulness. I was introduced to Ken through John Gardiner. John was a great supporter of Ken in his early career and when John opened his tennis ranches he named Ken as his touring professional. Ken would spend about sixty days a year in Arizona when he wasn't travelling the tennis circuit.

Ken and I became good friends. He and his wife, Wilma, would often join Marge and I for dinner and other social

Tennis star
Ken Rosewall—
a real class act

activities in Phoenix. We corresponded regularly even when tennis took Ken all around the world.

I'll never forget the summer of 1974 when Ken met Jimmy Connors in the final at Wimbledon. Connors was just emerging as a tennis superstar while Ken's career on the circuit was winding down. Even though Connors was victorious, it was a remarkable achievement for Ken just to reach the final.

Anyway, shortly after Wimbledon ended, we received a letter from Ken. It started like this: "I'm sitting here waiting to play Jimmy Connors in the finals of Wimbledon and I thought I'd write you a letter..." The letter was five pages long.

Can you imagine that! The stands at Wimbledon are packed, the fans are going crazy, and here is Ken Rosewall preparing for the biggest match of his life by sitting in the locker room and writing us a letter.

One year when Ken was playing in the Alan King tournament at Caesar's Palace in Las Vegas, he invited Marge and I to attend as his guests. We had seats for the early-round matches, the semi-finals and the finals. We were thrilled when Ken reached the finals.

During our stay in Vegas, we stayed at the Sands Hotel, just down the road from Caesar's Palace. On the morning of the finals, we decided to walk over to the tennis stadium after brunch. Ken said he'd have the tickets waiting for us.

I assumed the tickets would be left in our name at the will call booth. When we arrived at Caesar's Palace, standing outside with tickets in hand was none other than our gracious host, Ken Rosewall. He was dressed in his sweats waiting for us to arrive so he could personally hand us the tickets. He was so thoughtful, so gracious. Somehow, I can't imagine the spoiled tennis stars of today making such a fine gesture.

Now nearing sixty, Ken still competes today in Masters events around the world and wins most of his matches. The man from down under they affectionately call "Muscles" is a gentleman in every sense of the word.

My fighter:
Tony Doyle—The
Fighting Mormon

I always had a great love for the fight game, dating back to my Golden Gloves days in Paterson. The Paterson Armory was the scene of amateur, Golden Gloves, and professional fight cards every month. On fight night, I would park cars on the street, usually 17th Avenue. I would skip school, sit on the block and wait for everyone to arrive. They didn't have parking lots back then, so the neighborhood kids would park the cars for those people attending the fights. We were supposed to stay out and watch the cars while the fights were on, but we managed to sneak into the Armory to see what was going on. I served as the round boy during fights on many occasions.

One time, I witnessed a tragedy. Frankie Tenaro, a good local welterweight, died in the ring. I never want to witness that again. The referee waited too long to stop the fight. Frankie had a reputation to taking a good punch. This is one time his reputation did him in.

I was introduced to many of the influential people in the fight game and I guess it was only a matter of time before I had a fighter of my own. It took a while but I eventually had a taste of the fight game. After I had moved to Phoenix, I was approached by some people about backing a fighter from Salt Lake City named Irish Tony Doyle. With a name like that, how could I refuse?

I made one recommendation after agreeing to get involved in this venture. I stressed that it was essential to build up a record for Tony. That is, match him against some lesser fighters where he can get some wins and some confidence, before getting him a big fight. Unfortunately, this suggestion fell on deaf ears while Tony fell to the canvas.

I had to go to New York on business. One morning, I picked up the morning paper and immediately turned to the sports page, as I always did. Lo and behold, I noticed that in a fight in Philadelphia the previous night, Joe Frazier had knocked out Irish Tony Doyle in two rounds. So much for building up the record.

Despite this setback, I thoroughly enjoyed my association with Tony Doyle. We got him several fights in Chicago and—through my friendships with the sports columnists in town—we were able to get him plenty of exposure. I even persuaded one of my good friends, Dave Condon, sports editor of the _Chicago Tribune_, to become a second in the ring. We outfitted Dave in a white sweater covered with shamrocks. Tony, of course, had shamrocks all over his trunks and robe.

Before the Charley Singleton fight at the Aragon Ballroom in Chicago in 1970, Dave Condon approached me and said we had a problem. Dave had told his parish priest about his involvement and asked him to come down to wish Tony good luck. The good father went down to the dressing room to meet Tony as he was preparing for the fight. He asked Tony if he was nervous and Tony shook his head.

"Nevertheless," said the priest. "Perhaps it would be wise to kneel down and say a Hail Mary."

"I don't know what you're talking about," said Tony. "I'm a Mormon."

That was all Dave Condon needed to hear. He was dumbfounded.

"How could we put a Mormon in the ring with shamrocks all over him and deceive the public?" wondered Dave. "Do we introduce him as: Irish Tony Doyle, the fighting Mormon?"

It was a lot of fun owning a fighter. It was a hobby I managed to keep from my wife, Marge, until one night she got a call at our home in Scottsdale.

The person on the line says: "I'm Mickey Doyle—Tony's father."

Marge responds: "Who the hell is Tony Doyle?"

"He's Jack's fighter," says Mickey. "Tell him he needs an athletic supporter and send $100 as quickly as you can."

Try as I might, I could never keep some things from Marge. Of course, had I told her I may never have become involved in the fight game. It was an experience I wouldn't have missed for the world.

Who said long distance relationships don't work out? I have enjoyed a wonderful relationship with Grossinger Motors of Chicago for many years now.

You see, when I lived in Chicago, I drove nothing but General Motors' cars. When I first moved there, my neighbor was Gerry Schulte, the zone manager for the Pontiac Division of General Motors. We became friends and I went to Gerry every time I was about to buy a car.

Once he sent me to Grossinger's, who was his biggest dealer. In fact, they were one of the largest GM dealers anywhere. Paul Grossinger looked after me and treated me very well. When Paul died, he was succeeded by his brother Irwin. We became good friends and I always took my business to him.

Even after we moved to Arizona, I continued to buy my cars from Grossinger Motors in Chicago. Irwin would always arrange for someone to drive the car out to Scottsdale. Talk about going that extra mile for their customer! That's taking it to the extreme.

Irwin and I have become very close over the years and he

has invested in many of my real estate dealings in Arizona. I'm happy to report that they were all very successful ventures.

That's the way business worked back then. Not only did you become a customer, you became a friend and a partner. In fact, I still wear the wristwatch Irwin gave me in appreciation of one of our successful deals in Arizona.

Whoever said business was cutthroat was way off base. It can be fun and it creates friendships, too.

The mind of a sales-oriented person and the mind of an accountant can run on the same course, but in opposite directions. Confused? Let me explain.

Recently, I ran into a problem with a person going in the opposite direction. I submitted some minor expenses for travel. I also included some long-distance phone calls on the expense form.

"Why the phone calls?" inquired the guy with the pencil.

I told him that one of the calls was to the tax office and the others were return calls to people who responded to our 'available property' sign and called my number.

"Don't return the calls," urged the accountant. "Maybe they will call back."

"Maybe they won't," I said. "And, maybe one of those calls was a good prospect. It has happened before."

I'm still not sure if the pencil pusher got my point. But, that's precisely what I mean by two people on the same course going in the opposite direction.

To reiterate, I became involved in the real estate business almost by accident. All it took was a little comment by Harold Mayer to spark my interest. It was a great ride through the 1970s and early 1980s when our investments paid off handsomely. Here is a recap of some of the sweet deals.

1. Elliot Road—Tempe, Ariz. Moeur Ranch—Scottsdale, Ariz. (Total of 320 acres)

Date of purchase:	May 1968
Purchase price:	$640,000
Purchased from:	Valley Bank Trust Dept.
Resale date:	August 1975
Sale price:	$3,400,000
Sold to:	Dayton-Hudson
Gross profit:	$2,760,000

*This property was purchased with Harold Mayer. Harold had 50 percent and I had the remainder, along with 24 partners.

2. Flagstaff Investment Co.—Flagstaff, Ariz. (160 acres)

Date of purchase:	November 1968
Purchase price:	$160,500
Purchased from:	Michael Sanson Group
Resale date:	August 1975
Sale price:	$235,000
Sold to:	Bill Johnston
Gross profit:	$74,500

3. Scottsdale Site—Scottsdale, Ariz.
    (58,000 sq. ft.)

Date of purchase: February 1969
Purchase price: $41,000
Purchased from: Tom Van Sickel
Resale date: May 1976
Sale price: $105,000
Sold to: Mr. and Mrs. Richard Halleman
Gross profit: $63,500

4. Equestrian Manor—Scottsdale, Ariz.
    (140 acres)

Date of purchase: May 1969
Purchase price: $400,000
Purchased from: The Robert Aste Estate
Resale date: May 1973
Sale price: $1,000,000
Sold to: Tom Chauncey
Gross profit: $600,000

*Please note that we made money on the land, but lost $2 million on the development. Tom Chauncey bought the property after it was developed. You can't win them all.

5. Fort Valley Investment Company—Flagstaff, Ariz.
    (70 acres)

Date of purchase: May 1971
Purchase price: $70,000
Purchased from: Mike Sanson Group
Resale date: March 1973
Sale price: $250,000
Sold to: Thomas Gillard, president
                      Brent Offerman, vice-president
Gross profit: $180,000

6. Hardy & Knox—Tempe, Ariz.
   (26 acres)

Date of purchase:	May 1974
Purchase price:	$1,250,000
Purchased from:	Analease Corporation
	Alex Crutchfield
Resale date:	November 1976
Sale price:	$3,000,000
Sold to:	Dunlop & Magee
Gross profit:	$1,750,000

7. Scottsdale "20"—Scottsdale, Ariz.
   (20 acres)

Date of purchase:	March 1976
Purchase price:	$250,000
Purchased from:	Tom Chauncey/KOOL
Resale date:	April 1978
Sale price:	$375,000
Sold to:	Maloff Brothers
Gross profit:	$125,000

8. Prescott Country Club—Prescott, Ariz.
   (6 lots)

Date of purchase:	March 1976
Purchase price:	$60,000
Purchased from:	Tom Chauncey/KOOL
Resale date:	December 1986
Sale price:	$86,200
Sold to:	Lots sold individually
Gross profit:	$26,200

9. Scottsdale Industrial Park—Scottsdale, Ariz.
   (14 lots)

Date of purchase:	May 1977
Purchase price:	$420,000
Purchased from:	Tom VanSickel
Resale date:	July 1978 through March 1979
Sale price:	$562,453
Sold to:	Lots sold individually
Gross profit:	$142,453

10. San Ysidro—San Ysidro, Calif.
    (7 acres)

Date of purchase:	February 1978
Purchase price:	$720,000
Purchased from:	Richard Darley & Group
Resale date:	April 1979
Sale price:	$1,300,000
Sold to:	Dr. Salganick
Gross profit:	$580,000

11. The Seven Corners—Tempe, Ariz.
    (80 acres)

Date of purchase:	June 1978
Purchase price:	$2,200,000
Purchased from:	Arnold Goodman
Resale date:	August 1981
Sale price:	$5,011,552
Sold to:	4 lots sold individually
	3 lots sold to one buyer
Gross profit:	$2,811,552

12. The Chandler III—Chandler, Ariz.
     (32 acres)

Date of purchase: May 1982
Purchase price: $1,922,505
Purchased from: Edward B. Juliber for the William Miles, Jr.
                       and Almon S. Fish, Jr. Trust. Ben Tuttle,
                       Escrow Officer for Security Title Agency
Resale date: November 1985
Sale price: $3,000,000
Sold to: Conley Wolfswinkel
Gross profit: $1,077,495

13. Phoenix Plus 10—Phoenix, Ariz.
     (10 acres)

Date of purchase: February 1981
Purchase price: $500,000
Purchased from: Robert W. Edwards
Resale date: May 1984
Sale price: $1,100,000
Sold to: 75th & Cactii Associates, Chuck O. Lee
Gross profit: $600,000

14. McClintock & Ray—Tempe, Ariz.
     (15 acres)

Date of purchase: September 1981
Purchase price: $935,000
Purchased from: Drinkwater Group
Resale date: May 1984
Sale price: $1,600,000
Sold to: Conley Wolfswinkel (Pacific Scenes)
Gross profit: $665,000

15. Warner & McClintock—Tempe, Ariz.
    (10 acres)

Date of purchase: September 1981
Purchase price: $623,000
Purchased from: Drinkwater Group
Resale date: February 1984
Sale price: $1,300,000
Sold to: Dr. Edward B. Diethrich
Gross profit: $677,000

16. Rural & Ray Road—Tempe, Ariz.
    (15 acres)

Date of purchase: September 1981
Purchase price: $935,000
Purchased from: Drinkwater Group
Resale date: September 1983
Sale price: $1,650,000
Sold to: Conley Wolfswinkel (Pacific Scenes)
Gross profit: $715,000

Certainly these deals turned out quite well, but I was just one of several partners in these transactions. I put up my share of the deal in hard dollars. I was responsible for finding the property, handling the property and selling the property. We divided the profits among all my partners. I never bought anything on my own—I always had partners.

My friends knew me as a guy from Chicago working in the publishing business. It was easy for them to say, "what the hell does he know about real estate?" The best approach was to go in with equal shares. I'd get my friends involved in the venture, manage the property, look after the taxes, and then look for a buyer.

However, I did see changes coming and I advised all of my investors that there would be no more land purchases for a while. Nobody was hurt. John Morrissey, former Ford Motor Company executive and a great supporter of our land purchases, said in a letter: "That's the smartest move you've made, Jack. You advised us when it was good to go and when it was shaky to stop. Thanks."

Business turned sour with the announcement of the Savings and Loan (S & L) scandals and the Charles Keating stories. People became aware that everything was not in order in Washington, D.C. With this scandal ready to break, our politicians formed the Resolution Trust Corporation (RTC). In my opinion, they staffed it with less than competent leaders. The S & L investors had to be compensated and, these showboat executives lived in the lap of luxury for years before anyone caught on. Oh, the poor taxpayer.

When the RTC took over, it was little help. Granted, they rid themselves of property, but at bargain basement prices. The expense of handling these sales was horrendous. And, what did it do to the real estate investor? It lowered all values. Why pay a competitive price when you can buy distressed merchandise? It also lowered the price of comparable property. If land was valued at $3 a square foot and the RTC—for a quick sale—is selling a comparable, contiguous parcel for $1 that became the market value, even though the adjoining property is free and clear.

I also know of land owners who have reneged on their loan and had the RTC take over the property. Who did they resell it to? None other than the original owners for a lot less than they owed. We lost out and the people who re–purchased their land took credit for being good business people.

When are we going to get smart? Where is young Neil Bush? Ask him how business is in Colorado. He took the U.S. for a bundle and all he received for his actions was a slap on the wrist. Stealing four hubcaps will earn hard time for someone without clout.

Does this upset me? You bet your last dollar it does! I have often been accused of being too opinionated. That doesn't bother me in the least. I always maintained that one has to stand up for what he thinks and what he believes in.

What deeply concerns me is that in a country of 250 million people, the great wealth is owned and handled by too few. That, to me, is not democracy. That is not we, the people, speaking. Money talks and it filters down through the courts, the Senate, the House. As they say on the street: "Money talks and bullshit walks." There is plenty of truth in that statement.

11

Well, You Can Kiss My Shamrock

Family bonding is so important these days. A few years back, the boys and I took this bonding issue to the limit. In fact, you might want to call what we did 'family branding.'

You see, after several years of deliberating, we all decided to have a tattoo branded on our backsides. We thought it would be a clever way of identifying ourselves in case of disaster. Being Irish, we chose a shamrock as our symbol of identification.

We set a date for this momentous occasion. Tim and I met at a tattoo parlor in San Diego while Jack, Mike and Kevin had the work done in Chicago. We had a gentleman's agreement not to inform our wives.

Naturally, I was quite silent about it. About six months later, Marge received a call from Mike's wife, Cathy.

"Have you noticed anything different about Spoose (the nickname the kids gave me)?" asked Cathy.

"No," replied Marge.

Cathy then suggested Marge take a closer look at my butt. Needless to say, silence prevailed in our household for the next couple of weeks. By the way, Marge correctly assumed I was the ring leader of this caper.

To be perfectly honest, the boys and I think this is the greatest thing we've ever done as a family unit. The wives, however, reserve judgment.

Mike, who works for NBC's Today Show as a features correspondent, couldn't keep his tattoo to himself. Shortly afterwards, he displayed his shamrock to his colleagues at NBC. He quickly became the butt of many on-air jokes.

"Have I got a car for you?"

The best-looking car in Chicago belonged to my friend, Benny Stein. He had a blue and white Cadillac convertible, complete with all the bells and whistles. The car was equipped with an electronic eye and Benny had a continental kit on the back, with the spare tire mounted on top. It was truly a magnificent car.

One day, Benny came to pick me up at the office and I was admiring his car. "What a nice car, Benny," I said.

"You like it—I'll sell it to you," said Benny.

I didn't respond. I just let the remark pass. I didn't know if Benny was serious or not.

A few days later, I'm sitting in the office and Benny comes up to see me:

"Your car's downstairs, Jack," said Benny. "I just bought my new one."

I didn't know how I was going to get out of this one.

"Geez, Ben," I said. "I can't buy your car right now. I still have my station wagon."

Benny said: "Let's go get it and I'll sell it for you."

One thing about Benny Stein—he had the power of persuasion. Before I knew it, we were headed to the nearest car dealership. Benny shows the car to the salesman and tells him we'd like to sell it. The salesman gives Benny a price and Benny responds with a shot on the arm and a firm reply: "No way—$1,500 more."

Benny got his way. Goodbye, wagon. Hello, Cadillac. This car was huge. It was longer than the house I was living in. Sooner or later, I would have to face the music. I couldn't very well hide the car from Marge.

I decided to ask one of my colleagues, Bud Redpath, to come over to the house for dinner. Bud had just been transferred to the Chicago office from St. Louis. I figured his presence at the house would take some of the attention away from my new purchase. We parked the Cadillac in the driveway and entered the house. Neither of us said a word about the car. However, it didn't take long until someone noticed.

"Whose car is in the driveway?" asked my son, Jack.

"It's ours, because that's our license plate," chimed in son, Mike.

Almost immediately, Marge looked out the window and saw the car. She never said a word until Bud left. When the time came, she made herself perfectly clear.

"Get that car out and get it out quickly," she demanded.

It was a Friday night and I told her I'd take care of it first thing Saturday morning. I arose early, jumped in the car and was on my way to a dealer on the south side of Chicago. About two blocks away from home, Wally Gibbs, who ran the Pure Oil service station on Green Bay Road, flagged me down.

"What's the problem?" I asked.

"You'd better go home," said Wally. "Marge called and has changed her mind."

Marge was clever—she knew the route I would be taking. I made the fastest U-turn you've ever seen and returned to the house. Turned out that Marge loved the car. The car had everything. It even had a high-powered spotlight that became Marge's personal favorite. She would cruise down the streets of Glencoe with the kids at night and shine the light into the neighbors' homes. At first, they had no idea who it was. They thought it was the police until they finally learned it was Marge.

The car was truly one-of-a-kind. It became a real conversation piece and we had more fun with that car than any other car we owned. When I finally traded it in, I received more on the resale than I paid Benny.

Life is one great learning experience and I learned a lesson I wouldn't soon forget in the fall of 1957. Through various connections, I was able to acquire a number of tickets for the World Series between the Milwaukee Braves and the New York Yankees. I had many friends with the Braves, including club president Joe Cairns. In all, I had about fifty-six tickets and believe me, tickets were scarce. I gave them to customers, sales reps and friends.

As the Series went along, it began to lose a little of its lustre. By the final game in Milwaukee, I still had quite a few tickets left. Between commuting from Chicago to Milwaukee and staying overnight, I had spent a fair bit of money on these excursions. Bud Redpath, manager of _Life_ in Chicago, drove up with me for the game. When we arrived at County Stadium, I said to Bud: "Here's your ticket. I've got to discuss some business with someone. I'll meet you inside."

What I really wanted to do was to unload some tickets. The tickets were $7 each and I had a bunch left over. So there I was, standing outside the gate with the spare tickets in my pocket. Before long, I was approached by a gentleman.

"Do you have any extra tickets?" he asked.

"Yes, I do," I replied.

"Could you sell me a couple?"

"Sure."

"How much do you want?"

"Ten dollars apiece."

With that last remark, the man pulled out his badge and told me to come with him. I was mortified. I had not even taken the tickets out of my pocket. I was just talking to him.

But, what really concerned me was word of this episode getting back to the Braves. After all, I had received the tickets from the president of the club.

I managed to talk my way out of this dilemma and, fortunately, nobody associated with the Braves heard about it. It was my first and last experience with scalping. Nobody had to tell me not to do it again. Ironically, I was caught scalping at a Braves' game. Incidentally, Bud Redpath never found out about the incident. When I got back to my seat, I told him the business deal fell through.

Nyet, nyet!

I loved going to track meets. Track is such an individual sport and it requires so much dedication and training. These athletes are so talented and—in my opinion—they don't get nearly the recognition they deserve.

Speaking of recognition, at the annual *Daily News* relays meet at Chicago Stadium in 1964, I received far more than I deserved. That year, I took my sons, Jack and Mike, to the meet. Our seats were up quite high but afforded us a great view of the proceedings.

The main event of the night would be the men's mile. The event—called the Bankers' Mile—featured a great miler from Loyola of Chicago named Tom O'Hara. That night, O'Hara would set an indoor mile record with a time of 3:56.4.

The great thing about a track meet is that so much is

happening at once. You have to be very alert to catch everything that is going on.

The emcee of the meet was John Carmichael, sports editor of the *Daily News*. He served in that capacity for many years. Anyway, John is making an announcement of some sort. I'm not paying much attention to it. I just assumed he was announcing the starting time of the next event or calling the runners to the line. He was going on for some time.

However, what John was doing was giving a grand introduction for the Russian track coach, who was in attendance at the meet. He was detailing his background and his outstanding accomplishments.

I spotted a friend in the crowd and I stood up and started waving at him to get his attention. At that very moment, John Carmichael says, "And, there he is now." The huge spotlight turns on me to catch me waving to my friend.

I had been mistakenly identified as the Russian coach. Once I realized this, I quickly sat down. But, it was too late. There was no getting out of this one.

For the next month, at least, I was reminded of this faux pas whenever I walked down Michigan Avenue. There must have been 100,000 people in the Stadium that night for as many comments as I received. I knew just what they were muttering under their collective breath: "Now, the son of a bitch is taking bows for the Russians!"

They say the key to the success of a business is location, location, location. I might want to amend that statement to say: parking, parking, parking.

I became involved in a restaurant venture in Chicago in the 1960s. We opened up a deli on Wabash Avenue called Stanley Green's. A fellow named Sid Lovitt from Providence knew of a very successful deli on Chestnut Street in Philadelphia by the same name. He thought the same formula would work in Chicago.

Sid was the major investor in the restaurant. I was a partner in the venture along with such friends as Jesse Owens, Danny O'Neil and Newt Minow. The restaurant

The front of Stanley Green's restaurant—great food, but where's the parking lot?

had a great atmosphere, but business was struggling. During the lunch hour, we were busy, but afterwards it was dead. It took us a while to figure it out, but finally we recognized the problem. We didn't have any parking at the restaurant. Had we done any market research, maybe we would have identified the problem.

One night, we had a meeting with our accountant who outlined the restaurant's dire financial situation. Finally, Sid Lovitt said in a low voice: "I think it's time for a grease fire."

Sid was only kidding, of course, but one should never kid about something like that. Needless to say, it wasn't long before Stanley Green's closed its doors for good.

It was not a huge investment, but nobody likes a loser. Stanley Green's provided us with a lot of laughs, but it was a financial disaster.

Who says you can't have a little fun while at church? I'm not sure why but our family seemed to have more than our share of laughs at Sacred Heart Church in Hubbard Woods, a section of Winnetka, Ill.

The pastor at the church was Monsignor Hillenbrand, a very holy and learned man. My sons began to serve Mass under Monsignor Hillenbrand on weekday mornings. They found out quickly he was very strict and no nonsense would be tolerated.

One day, while my son Jack was serving Mass, the phone started to ring outside the sanctuary. The ringing was loud and clear throughout the church. Monsignor Hillenbrand had his back to the congregation as was customary in those days. He quietly told Jack to go answer the phone. Jack didn't hear him or pretended not to hear him. He asked him a second time, only in a louder voice: "I said, go answer the phone!"

Jack didn't move. Monsignor Hillenbrand was clearly angered. Finally, he barks out: "Go answer the phone!" The command is audible to everyone. Jack left the altar and went to answer it. A short time later, he returned and announced to Monsignor Hillenbrand: "It's for you!"

That story made the rounds in Winnetka for years and years. For the longest time, Jack was known as the kid who tried to get Monsignor Hillenbrand to answer the phone in church.

Monsignor Hillenbrand was responsible for organizing the ushers at church. Five ushers were assigned to each Mass— one at 8:00 A.M.; one at 9:00 A.M.; one at 10:00 A.M.; another at 11:00 A.M. and so forth.

One team of ushers included a fellow named Bill Corbett. Bill loved to usher, but he had some genuine fears about the job, as he confessed to Marge at a party one night. Bill told Marge his biggest fear was someone fainting in church or, worse yet, someone throwing up in church.

That was all she needed to hear. Next time she was out shopping, she stopped at a novelty store and purchased one of those fake vomit patches. You know, the ones made of plastic that you throw on the floor.

Marge kept it in her purse for the next time she was in church. There was a full house in church that day and, sure enough, Bill Corbett was on duty. Marge discreetly placed the plastic vomit patch under the pew in front of her.

She turned around and motioned to Bill. He came over and she pointed to the problem under the seat. He muttered, "Son of a bitch." Off he went.

He returned with a bucket of water and a mop. He cleared everyone out of the pew, dipped the mop and gave it a splash. When the plastic moved, Bill was livid. He chased Marge down the aisle and out the back of the church.

Marge had a great reputation for practical jokes. She could put on that innocent face and keep the victim guessing for hours. Believe me, it was a long time before Bill Corbett forgave her for that incident in church.

JACK LEONARD _____

12

Time Flies When You're Having Fun

As we approach the end of the century, I must admit I lived in a special era. I was born at a great time.

As a child, I can remember putting the sign in the window for the ice man or the milk man to stop at the house. And, they made their deliveries by horse and wagon.

I vaguely remember the end of World War I and, of course, have vivid memories of serving my country in World War II. To go from a horse and buggy to a man on the moon is a remarkable evolution. I've witnessed the rise of the automobile, the age of television and the rapid advances in high technology. Not everybody can make that claim.

I've lived during a good time. Anybody younger than fifty can't relate to the non-television days. I can recall my father making a radio in the kitchen with a Quaker Oats box, a crystal, cat hair and ear phones. With that contraption, we were able to pick up station KDKA in Pittsburgh.

Indeed, I've been fortunate. Nothing more could happen than what I've seen in my lifetime.

The Leonard clan at our fiftieth anniversary party in 1993

It's been a long and eventful journey from Paterson, N.J. to La Jolla, Calif. The ride has had its share of ups and downs, but I've always said you've got to take the good with the bad. I must admit I'm glad I jumped aboard for the ride. And, I'm also thankful that my mother and father did not miss the boat.

I'll always cherish my days at Time Inc. It was a special place, a special time in my life. I knew I was blessed to work for such great people in such a wonderful environment. But, it wasn't until after I left the company that I truly began to appreciate its greatness. Once you have seen the other side of the picture—for example, working at Curtis Publishing and for the City of Phoenix—you begin to realize the unique qualities of a place like Time Inc.

Of course, everyone needs a little variety and I've had my share. To wit: Partner in a Chicago restaurant (Stanley Greens), part owner of a minor league baseball team (Phoenix Giants Triple A club), affiliated with a minor league hockey club (Phoenix Roadrunners), owner of a professional boxer (Irish Tony Doyle, the Fighting Mormon) and investor/partner in real estate and land development (Arizona and California).

Some of these business ventures worked out, some of them didn't, but I don't regret the experience for a minute. Despite the bumps, it was a good ride and thoroughly enjoyable.

Nevertheless, there are times when I wonder if I would have been better off remaining in Paterson. Sure, the path I chose afforded me the opportunity to meet interesting people from all walks of life. But, would I have been just as content living a simple and uncomplicated life? Probably.

I do know that growing up in Paterson gave me perspective and prepared me for life's rocky road. Back in Paterson, if someone in need asked you for a donation, the hand went in the pocket and, if you had it, you helped them out. Today, if you went to the suburbs and asked the same question, the reply would be: "Is it tax deductible?" It says a lot about people and their value system.

To the boys, if I could offer you one piece of advice, it would be this: Follow your conscience and your beliefs. Be good to yourself and your family. That's what is important and, to me, that's what life is all about.

And, to Marge, I know it hasn't been easy. But, you always said it was an exciting ride and you helped steer me on the right course.

It really has been the time of my life. Thanks.

Index

A

Abbott, Bud   13
Ainslie, Jim   25, 84
Albo, Marge   159
Albo, Robert   158
Allen, George   85
Andrews, Admiral
    Adolphus   18, 21
Antosz, Henry   139
Armstrong, Libby   30
Aste, Bob   147
Aste, Peggy   147

B

Baer, Buddy   18
Banks, Fatty   11
Barr, Don   51
Barr, William   129
Baucher, Red   107
Bavasi, Buzzie   136, 137
Becker, Gary   61
Bennett, Tony   136
Benton, Bill   99
Bentsen, Lloyd   157
Biondi, Frank   157
Black, Howard   2,
    55, 65, 79, 84
Block, Henry   157
Borgeman, Bennie   11
Boros, Julius   88
Breslin, Jake   12
Brumbaugh, Dave   26, 27,
    55, 102
Bryant, Paul "Bear"   91
Buckhout, Clay   2, 65, 70
Burchtold, Bill   121

Burnett, Leo   98, 126
Burtis, Allan   23
Bush, Neil   176
Butts, Wally   91
Byrnes, Bob   119

C

Cairns, Joe   181
Calloway,
    Llewelleyn "Pete"   69, 73
Carmichael, John   183
Cascino, Tony   99
Castellini, Bob   157
Charles, Ezzard   115
Chauncey, Tom   150
Colt, Alex   60
Colvin, Don   127
Condon, Dave   166
Cone, Fairfax   98
Connors, Jimmy   162
Corbett, Bill   186
Costello, Lou   13
Crown, Henry   132
Crown, Lester   132
Crown, Renee   132
Culligan, Joe   95, 97, 98, 100
Curran, Bill   61

D

Dacosse, Gene   139
dal Bianco, Bruno   133
Daley, Richard   43, 134
Daly, Bill   78
Daugherty, Red   63, 69
Davey, Chuck   92

DeGrazia, Michael   154
Diehl, George   15
Dillingham, Bob   66
Ditka, Mike   86
Donnelly, Johnny   139
Douglas, Mike   136
Doyle, Irish Tony   165
Doyle, Mickey   166
Duchin, Eddy   141
Duchin, Peter   142
Durkin, Bill   13

E

Eagen, Msgr I. B.   56
Evans, Chick   51

F

Faeber, Harry   25, 102
Farley, James A.   37
Fats, Minnesota   130
Flood, T. Patrick   151
Flores, Chi Chi   140
Foss, Barbara   154
Foss, Heinie   154
Frank, Clint   72, 123
Frazier, Joe   165
Frye, Phil   156
Fuchs, Jim   97
Fullmer, Gene   80

G

Gallagher, Dennis   143
Galvin, Robert   157
Gardiner, Barbara   156
Gardiner, John   133, 154, 161

Gart, Murray   56
Gibbs, Wally   180
Gleason, Jackie   130
Goldberg, Marshall   72
Gram (Margaret
    Hattersley)   101
Graziano, Rocky   92
Griffin, Merv   136, 158
Grossinger, Irwin   167
Grossinger, Paul   167
Guevera, Lou   140
Gunderson, Les   107

H

Hadden, Brit   63
Hadden, Pete   63, 69
Hagan, John   154
Hagan, Marjorie   154
Halas, George   72
Hanrahan, Don   61
Hanson, Chuck   1, 65, 70
Hayes, Woody   89
Heiskell, Bob   2
Henrich, Tommy   82
Hesburgh, Ted   131
Higgins, Eddie   156
Higgins, Harold   156
Hillenbrand, Msgr.   185, 186
Hitler, Adolf   105
Hollings, Ernest   157
Holman, Bill   59
Howlett, Phil   124
Hull, Bobby   81

I

Ivan, Tommy   77

J

Jackson, C.D. 55
James, Sid 2, 62
Jencke, Lt. Ernest Lee 19
Jensen, Roger 151
Jordan, Michael 87

K

Keane, Bil 159
Keating, Charles 175
Kelley, Steve 64
Kelly, Bill 61, 66, 76
Kennedy, Ethel (Skakel) 119
Kennedy, John 95, 116
Kennedy, Robert 117, 119, 120
King, Alan 158
King, Ed 52
Kirby, Clarke 141
Knell, Frank 147
Kroc, Ray 54

L

Lacey, Fred 84, 128
Laguerre, Andre 71
LaMotta, Jake 121
Lapchick, Joe 11
Larsen, Roy 2, 38, 55
Lawler, Joe Joe 26
Lee, Sammy 44
Leonard, Cathy 134, 177
Leonard, Jack 30, 82, 101,
    112, 133, 177, 179, 182, 185
Leonard, Kevin 47, 101, 177
Leonard, Marge 3, 9, 30, 41,
    101, 158, 161, 177, 179, 186, 192

Leonard, Mary 8
Leonard, Mike 82, 101,
    133, 177, 179, 182
Leonard, Nancy 8
Leonard, Thomas 8
Leonard,
    Thomas Joseph 5, 9, 42
Leonard, Tim 3, 101,
    112, 133, 177
Lewis, Ralph 32
Linen, Jim 63
Louis, Joe 18
Love, Fred 52, 53
Love, George 53
Love, Jim 53
Lovitt, Sid 184
Luce, Harry 2, 51, 68, 75
Luckman, Sid 72, 85, 123
Lytle, Don 53

M

Malloy, Art 14
Mantle, Mickey 45
Marciano, Rocky 115
Marconi, Joe 87
Marsh, Bruce 61, 124
Maule, Tex 62
Mayer, Alan 147
Mayer, Harold 123, 145,
    147, 156, 169
Mayer, June 145
McCormick, Pat 44
McDaniel, Captain 141
McKinney, Captain 22
McLoone, John 154
McShane, Jimmy 95, 115, 119
Meredith, James Howard 118

S

Saban, Lou   89
Salinger, Pierre   96
Schulte, Gerry   167
Schwartz, Izzie   12
Shaughnessy, Clark   72
Shiel, Bishop   46, 126
Shields, Midgey   13
Shore, Dinah   34
Singleton, Charley   166
Skelton, Red   14
Skinnell, Tom   65
Smith, Annie   5, 121
Snyder, Larry   110
Sperry, Don   61, 66
Stein, Benny   121, 178
Stillman, Charlie   2, 29, 31,
   32, 33, 39, 68, 102
Stirnweiss, George "Snuffy"   82
Stoneham, Mary   128
Stydahar, Joe   71, 85, 123
Suydam, Hank   116
Sutherland, Jim   36
Swan, Jim   66

T

Tax, Jeremiah   62
Tenaro, Frankie   165
Thompson, Page   86
Thorson, Roger   64
Tower, Whitney   62

V

Van Brocklin, Norm   72
Veronis, John   97

W

Wallace, Nick   2, 35,
   39, 55, 142
Warner, John   157
Weischaar, Father Michael   161
Welles, Sam   77
Wells, Sid   121
White, Jim   97
White, Margaret Bourke   125
Willey, Doug   153
Willey, June   153
Williams, Edward Bennett   86
Wilson, Kenneth "Tug"   109
Winchell, Walter   18
Wooley, Doc   27
Wright, Mickey   88
Wrigley, P.K.   153

The Time of My Life
About the Authors

Jack Leonard spent nearly a quarter of a century at Time Inc. in New York and Chicago. It was an experience he wouldn't have missed for the world. Starting out in the corporate production department, Jack worked his way up to be Midwest manager of *Sports Illustrated* in Chicago. Along the way, there were some ups and downs, but always lots of laughs.

Born in Paterson, N.J. in 1916, Jack attended Mount Saint Mary's College in Emmitsburg, Md. before joining the Navy in 1941. After his discharge from the service in 1945, he had a brief stay at The Great Atlantic & Pacific Tea Company before landing at Time Inc. A most eventful career in the publishing industry ensued.

After retiring from Time Inc. in Chicago, the Leonard clan moved to Arizona where Jack began a second career in real estate development. He is still involved in several real estate ventures in Arizona.

Jack and his wife Marge now reside in La Jolla, Calif.

Co-author Sid Shapira is a transplanted Canadian, now living in San Diego. Born in Winnipeg, Sid attended Ryerson Polytechnical Institute in Toronto, where he graduated with his degree in journalism in 1979. Sid worked as a reporter for daily newspapers in both Toronto and Winnipeg.

Over the past few years, Sid has worked as a public relations and marketing specialist. Not long after moving to Southern California, he met Jack Leonard and was fascinated by his many stories about the good old days at Time Inc.

When Jack approached him about the prospect of collaborating on this autobiography, Sid jumped at the chance. Writing this book, he says, has been a wonderful experience.